Oliver Huntington Richardson

The National Movement in the Reign of Henry III. and its Culmination in the Barons' War

Oliver Huntington Richardson

The National Movement in the Reign of Henry III. and its Culmination in the Barons' War

ISBN/EAN: 9783337012311

Printed in Europe, USA, Canada, Australia, Japan

Cover: Foto ©ninafisch / pixelio.de

More available books at **www.hansebooks.com**

THE NATIONAL MOVEMENT

IN THE

REIGN OF HENRY III.

AND ITS

CULMINATION IN THE BARONS' WAR

BY

OLIVER H. RICHARDSON, A.B.
PROFESSOR OF HISTORY IN DRURY COLLEGE

New York
THE MACMILLAN COMPANY
LONDON: MACMILLAN & CO., LTD.
1897

All rights reserved

COPYRIGHT, 1896,
BY OLIVER H. RICHARDSON.

Norwood Press
J. S. Cushing & Co. — Berwick & Smith
Norwood Mass. U.S.A.

To My Wife

PREFACE

THIS book does not represent an attempt to rewrite the history of the beginnings of parliamentary government in England, nor does it contain an exhaustive account of the political history of the reign of Henry III. Its object is to portray, first, those movements which tended to denationalize the church and state of England by the perversion of the English constitution and by the introduction of the political doctrines of thirteenth-century France and the Empire-Church; and second, those counter-movements which resulted in the complete triumph of the national principle as manifested in the dim beginnings of the revolt from Rome, in the completion of race unity, and the establishment of the constitution upon a basis both national and popular. The literature of the period is both copious and picturesque, as befits an epoch in which the personality of the actors has unusual weight, and in which the study of motive is of unusual importance. If the author has been enabled to catch the spirit of the time from the pages of the historians who lived among the events which they so vividly describe, his object will have been accomplished.

HEIDELBERG, GERMANY, Aug. 12, 1896.

LIST OF AUTHORS AND EDITIONS CITED

Bartholomæi de Cotton. Historia Anglicana. Ed. Luard. Rolls Series, 1859.
Benedictus Abbas Petroburgensis. Ed. Thos. Stapleton. Camden Society, 1849.
Blaauw, W. H. The Barons' War. London and Lewes, 1844.
Böhmer, Joh. Fried. Regesta Imperii. Stuttgart, 1844.
Calendarium Rotulorum Patentium. London, 1802.
Fabyan, Robert. The New Chronicles of England and France. Ed. Hen. Ellis. London, 1811.
Fiske, John. The Beginnings of New England. Boston.
Freeman, E. A. History of the Norman Conquest of England. Oxford, 1876.
Gardiner and Mullinger. English History for Students. New York, 1881.
Gneist, R. Englische Verfassungsgeschichte. Berlin, 1882.
Green, J. R. History of the English People. London, 1877.
Grosseteste, Roberti, Epistolæ. Ed. Luard. Rolls Series, 1861.
Guizot, M. Histoire des Origines du Gouvernement Représentatif. Paris, 1851.
Chronica Johannis de Oxenedis. Ed. Sir Henry Ellis. Rolls Series, 1859.
Chronicon de Lanercost. Bannatyne Club. Edinburgh, 1839.
Lanfranci Opera. Ed. Giles. Oxford and Paris, 1844.
Liber de Antiquis Legibus. Ed. Thos. Stapleton. Camden Society, 1846.
Lingard, John. History of England. 4th ed. Paris, 1826.
Chronica de Mailros. Bannatyne Club. Ed. J. Stevenson. Edinburgh, 1835.
Matthæi Pariensis Chronica Majora. Ed. Luard. Rolls Series, 1872–1882.
Matthæus Westmonasteriensis. Flores Historiarum. Frankfort, 1601.

Migne. Patrologia Latina. (T. 159.)
Annales Monastici. Ed. Luard. Rolls Series. 1864–1869.
    Vol. I. Annales de Theokesberia.
            Annales de Burton.
    Vol. II. Annales Monasterii de Wintonia.
            Annales Monasterii de Waverleia.
    Vol. III. Annales Prioratus de Dunstaplia.
    Vol. IV. Annales Monasterii de Oseneia.
            Chronicon Vulgo Dictum Chronicon Thomæ Wykes.
            Annales Prioratus de Wigornia.
Monumenta Franciscana. Ed. Brewer. Rolls Series, 1858.
    Pars I. Thomæ de Eccleston De Adventu Fratrum Minorum in Angliam.
    Pars II. Adæ de Marisco Epistolæ.
Nangis, Guillaume de. Chronique Latine. Ed. H. Géraud. French Hist. Soc. Paris, 1843.
Pauli, Reinhold.
    Bilder aus Alt-England. Gotha, 1876.
    Geschichte von England. Hamburg, 1853.
    Simon von Montfort, der Schöpfer des Hauses der Gemeinen. Tübingen, 1867.
    Tübinger Programm. Tübingen, 1864.
Pearson, C. H. History of England in the Early and Middle Ages. London, 1867.
Chronicon Petroburgense. Ed. Thos. Stapleton. Camden Society, 1849.
Von Raumer. Geschichte der Hohenstaufen und ihrer Zeit. 5th ed. Leipzig, 1878.
Raynaldus. Annales Ecclesiastici. (Mansi.) Lucca, 1747.
Rishanger, Wilhelmi, Monachi S. Albani, Chronica. Ed. Riley. Rolls Series, 1865.
    Continuatio Matthæi Parisiensis. Ed. Wats. London, 1640. (Earlier edition of the preceding.)
    Chronicon. Ed. Halliwell. Camden Society, 1840.
Robert of Gloucester's Chronicle. Ed. Hearne. London, 1810.
Rymer, Thomas. Fœdera, Conventiones, etc. Ed. Clarke and Holbrook. London, 1816.
Shirley. Royal and other Historical Letters, illustrative of the Reign of Henry III. Rolls Series. London, 1866.
Statutes of the Realm. 1810.

Stubbs, William.
  The Constitutional History of England. 5th ed. Clar. Press. Oxford, 1891.
  Select Charters, illustrative of English History. 8th ed. Clar. Press. Oxford, 1895.
Taswell-Langmead, T. P. English Constitutional History. London and Boston, 1886.
Trivet's Annales sex regum Angliæ. Ed. Hog. E. H. S. London, 1845.
Walteri de Hemingburgh, Chronicon. Ed. H. C. Hamilton. E. H. S. London, 1848.
Wood. Historia et Antiquitates Universitatis Oxoniensis. Oxford, 1674.
Wright, Thomas. Political Songs of England, from the Reign of John to that of Edward II. Camden Society, 1839.

CONTENTS

CHAPTER I

THE FORCES WHICH MADE ENGLAND A NATION IN THE REIGN OF HENRY III.

PART		PAGE
I.	Introduction: Primary Forces	1
II.	The Influence of the Friars	19

CHAPTER II

THE FORCES WHICH ROUSED ENGLAND TO ARMED RESISTANCE

I.	The Poetical Literature	36
II.	The Alienation of London from the Crown	42
III.	The Alienation of Simon de Montfort from the Crown	50
IV.	The Denationalization of England: the State	65
V.	The Denationalization of England: the Church and the Pope	84
VI.	The Denationalization of England: the Church and the King	105
VII.	The Sicilian Crown	113
VIII.	The Welsh War, and the Famine of the Year 1258	145

CHAPTER III

THE OUTBREAK: AND THE CULMINATION OF THE NATIONAL MOVEMENT

PART		PAGE
I.	The Reform Parliaments of the Year 1258	152
II.	The Government of the Barons: War and Peace	181
III.	Parties and Principles	203

CHAPTER I

THE FORCES WHICH MADE ENGLAND A NATION IN THE REIGN OF HENRY III.

PART I

Introduction: Primary Forces

THE reconciliation of individual freedom with social order is an ever-recurring problem whose solution has varied with each stage in the world's evolution and with the peculiar factors which constitute the life of different social groups. At the time of its inception, at least, feudalism was a form of government which allowed to the individual the maximum of personal liberty compatible with the maintenance of even tolerable order within the limits of the state and protection from foes outside its borders. It was the spontaneous and inevitable creation of the liberty-loving Teuton when confronted with forms of life more complex than those of his ancestral forests. Liberty tended to degenerate into license; the centrifugal forces of the social world to overcome the centripetal; and the natural outcome of unrestrained feudalism was practical social anarchy. Frequently, however, the force of the action engendered a reaction of corresponding magnitude, and a highly centralized form of government was the result.

William the Conqueror, after his experiences with the turbulent vassals of Normandy, was not likely to neglect in the establishment of his rule in England the vantage offered by the undefined prerogative of an English king. If feudalism was introduced into England by the Conquest as the result of repeated confiscations of the estates of all who refused to recognize him as the lawful successor of Edward the Confessor, it was introduced not so much as a system of government as a mode of land tenure, and the worst feature of continental feudalism was abolished by the anti-feudal law[1] of the Gemot of Salisbury Plain. The government of William I. and his immediate successor was practically despotic, but necessarily so; order in a government based in reality upon race-differences — however disregarded in theory — could be secured only through absolutism. The world-struggle between individual liberty, typified in England by Anglo-Saxon local customs, and good order, typified by royal supremacy, had entered in England upon a new phase.[2] Speaking broadly, from the accession of William I. to the loss of Normandy under John, good order was maintained by the union of crown and English people against the baronage, — but at the expense of liberty: from the loss of Normandy to the reign of Edward I.

---

[1] Stubbs' Select Charters, pp. 81, 82.
[2] Cf. Fiske's Beginnings of New England, chap. I.

liberty could be secured only by the union of barons and people against the crown, — but at the expense of good order. The road to permanent order *and* freedom led through the disorders of the Barons' War to the establishment of a parliamentary system. During the whole of this period the relation of the English church to the germinating constitution and to the Papal See was of paramount importance.

The character of the church in England had already been largely determined before the arrival of the Normans. Though abundantly grateful to the power which had founded and so carefully cherished it in its early days, — a gratitude evinced by the ready payment of Peter's pence, by the labours of many a missionary upon the continent, and in particular by the vast services of Winfred in favour of papal prerogative, — the church had been, nevertheless, at an early date stamped with the national seal. It is especially characteristic, that at a comparatively early period the sons of illustrious houses became enrolled among its members;[1] that the clergy, ecclesiastical having preceded political unity, speedily exercised a healing influence upon state affairs; then, later, as members of the witenagemot, influenced greatly the action of the central administration, while in the shire-moot, the highest organ of local government, the bishop exercised concurrent jurisdiction with the ealdorman. The clergy, composed of all classes in the community, identified com-

---

[1] Gneist's Englische Verfassungsgeschichte, p. 8.

pletely with the government of the state, and having as their especial duty the care of the weak and oppressed, naturally acquired a national feeling more profound than existed in any church upon the continent. Moreover, the See of Rome was too distant to raise effective claims to the immediate headship of a community which was neither accustomed nor inclined to separate authority from personal presence.[1]

To the attribute of nationality was therefore joined the attribute of an independence which was almost perfect as regarded the pope, less so with respect to the king.[2] In each case its basis was necessarily the strength afforded by national sympathies and popular support. The importance of this strong feeling of nationality existent in the English church before the Norman Conquest, and of the identity of interests established at that time between the masses of the clergy and the people, though too obvious to be overlooked, is too great not to be mentioned. Upon this thread hung the future liberties of England. The Norman Conquest, with all the changes which it introduced into the government of church and state, and into the mutual relations of church and state, never permanently shook this elemental force. Under the first sovereigns of Norman race, it was the best guarantee

---

[1] Gneist, Eng. Verf. Gesch., p. 29. Cf. Stubbs' Constitutional History, I., p. 267.

[2] For opposing views as to the king's share in the appointment of bishops, cf. Stubbs' Const. Hist., I., p. 150, and Gneist, pp. 29, 30. My indebtedness to these two authors, in this Introduction, demands a general acknowledgment.

against feudal anarchy; under Stephen, it emerged as the only organized power whose integrity had not suffered serious loss; under John, its alliance with the baronage offered the decisive check to royal absolutism.

While the church in Norman and Angevin England maintained close and on the whole friendly relations with Rome, it is evident that pope and church were by no means synonymous terms, and that the policy of the latter frequently ran directly counter to that of the former. For this Englishmen can scarcely be too thankful; in the great crises in which the popular liberties were at stake in its early history, the English church, almost uniformly, warmly championed the cause of freedom; papal authority at the most only succeeded in temporarily paralyzing its action, never in making it abjectly subservient. The first great crisis for papal power in England occurred in the latter days of Henry II. and John, terminating with a seeming papal victory; the religious crisis in John's reign blended with the political movement which evoked the Magna Charta and led to the critical periods of the reign of Henry III.; these were crises for English national existence and the English system of representation, and in them the pope was the steady antagonist of English liberty. That after victory he counselled moderation from motives of policy is the highest praise which he can rightly claim.[1]

---

[1] Gualo's case is only an apparent exception; during John's reign, Innocent had done his worst against English freedom, supporting the

The national character of the English church was preserved at the Conquest mainly through two causes: first, the bulk of the lower clergy remained Saxon and retained the Saxon speech, while their influence, largely expended in protecting the conquered race from the oppression of the nobles, necessarily became weightier and weightier as the fusion of races progressed; second, the admirable position of William I. and Lanfranc toward one another assured their joint resistance to unreasonable papal demands. Said William to Hubert, the legate sent by Gregory to request more regular payment of Peter's pence and to demand fealty, "The one claim I have admitted, the other I have not; I have refused to do homage and still refuse, because I have neither promised it myself, nor do I learn that my predecessors have done it to yours."[1] Upon this statesmanlike declaration and upon the first of his three celebrated canons,[2] William sought to assure the freedom of the church from Rome.

He himself remained its master, but on terms which his Angevin successors found themselves unable to maintain. Under William, ample security for the obe-

---

tyranny of a king whose power was largely based on foreign mercenaries; and if Honorius, through Gualo, helped to drive out Louis of France, it was with the intention of securing Henry's power. No one can doubt that the cassation of charters of liberty was more congenial to the popes than their confirmation.

[1] Lanfranci Opera, I., p. 32. For correspondence between Gregory and William, Lanfranc and Gregory, *vide* Freeman, Norman Conquest, IV., pp. 432–437.

[2] Eadmer, Hist. Nov. apud Sel. Chart., p. 82. Migne, Pat. Lat. T. 159, p. 351.

dience of the church was found in the necessity for the royal confirmation of the decrees of provincial synods; in the prohibition to excommunicate a crown-vassal or officer without the king's consent; in the establishment of the dual character of ecclesiastics as at once clerk and feudal vassal; and in the rigid supervision of episcopal elections.[1] The celebrated decree of separation,[2] however, by which bishops and archdeacons were forbidden to hold pleas in the hundred-court or to bring any matter pertaining to the cure of souls before a lay tribunal, but instead were ordered to establish courts of their own in which all cases were to be tried by ecclesiastical law, was full of danger. However admirable the mutual intentions of prelate and king, and however well adapted to the reforming spirit abroad in the church this measure might be, yet, as Pearson[3] expresses it, " When William I. and Lanfranc concurred in a policy which dissolved the old union of the two bodies politic, they had unavoidably placed them in a condition of suppressed antagonism." Such great concessions had been made to the church and in such vague language, that encroachments were sure to follow as soon as the state fell into weaker hands. The actual results of a century of separation were that the clergy found law and discipline in the canon law alone; their ideal, in separation from the laity; and that a strong party, especially among

---

[1] Sel. Chart., p. 82.
[2] Rymer, I., p. 3. Sel. Chart., p. 85.
[3] Pearson, I., p. 495.

the monks, stood decisively upon the side of Rome.[1] To the archbishop of Canterbury the papal confirmation became speedily as essential as the royal, and Innocent III. could successfully nominate Langton in defiance of John; the mode of election to bishoprics varied from the congé d'élire[2] of Henry II. to the absolute renunciation of royal right to interfere, contained in John's Charter[3] of Nov. 21, 1214; and in 1204, at the consecration of Peter des Roches, the pope "laid down the rule that where the electors have knowingly elected an unworthy person they lose the right of making the next election."[4] As the crown had already lost the right to determine contested elections, the appointment in such a case pertained to the pope.

Legatine authority also greatly increased, as well as the custom of appeals to Rome. During the turbulent reign of Stephen such encouragement had been given to papal interference and the clergy had become as a body so independent[5] of the king's control, that Henry II. found himself face to face with a most difficult problem. If the secular authority were not to become impotent, drastic measures must at once be taken. The result was the Becket controversy.

---

[1] Gneist, Eng. Verf. Gesch., p. 193.
[2] Sel. Chart., p. 140, cap. XII.
[3] *Ibid.*, pp. 288, 289.
[4] Stubbs' Const. Hist., III., 313.
[5] From Stephen's second Charter, Sel. Chart., p. 120. Ecclesiasticarum personarum et omnium clericorum et rerum eorum justitiam et potestatem et distributionem bonorum ecclesiasticorum in manu episcoporum esse perhibeo et confirmo.

Undoubtedly the Constitutions of Clarendon contained the true statement of English law and English custom, and as such were accepted by barons and bishops, — by all, that is, except Becket and his immediate followers, the monks. Henry's glorious victory, however, was ruined by his own precipitation and rashness; Becket's murder was followed by a popular reaction, and the king was forced to the double humiliation of Canterbury and Avranches.[1] Appeals to Rome were henceforward allowed, and no clerk, though convicted of crime, was to be summoned before a temporal judge. Important in form as these concessions were, other consequences still more important resulted indirectly from this struggle. First, a limit had been set to the royal absolutism. Second, Henry's attention had been drawn from foreign affairs, and his whole strength confined to England, at exactly that moment when projects of foreign conquest must have seemed, and were, most feasible. The acquisition of Poitou and Guienne through the marriage with Eleanor was fated to cause England a sufficiency of suffering in the reign of Henry III.; it may well be that the controversy with Becket prevented England from sinking into the position of a French subject-province. In a certain sense, therefore, if this conjecture be allowed to stand, the controversy must be ranked as analogous to the loss of Normandy in helping to make England, England. Third, to resist the

---

[1] Benedictus Abbas, pp. 34–36. For practical result, *vide* Green, History English People, I., p. 178.

archbishop successfully, the king had been forced to call upon the baronage for support; and to resist the Canon Law, Anglo-Saxon institutions and customs had been cited :[1] the appeal ultimately proved dangerous to the crown, — memories of the witenagemot were stirred in the minds of its higher vassals, the lower baronage began to find community of interests with Saxon free-holders, and after Normandy had been lost and race-fusion fairly begun, the movement culminated in the Magna Charta.[2]

Reference has been already made[3] to the connection of the religious crises of Henry II. and John with the political crises of the same monarchs and Henry III. As early as 1204 by the appointment of Peter des Roches as bishop of Winchester, and again, still more unmistakably, two years later by the method of Langton's election, Innocent III. had defined his position toward the independence of the English church; it was reserved for following years to display in its fulness his baleful influence upon English popular liberties.

But while the pope was posing as the champion of despotism, England reaped the benefit of possessing a church long the depository of constitutional law, and which was national and independent by heredity. If bishop Roger of Salisbury had been the creator of constitutional machinery, Stephen Langton, archbishop

---

[1] *Vide* Preamble to Constitutions of Clarendon, Sel. Chart., pp. 137, 138.

[2] Pauli, Simon von Montfort, pp. 2, 3.   [3] *Supra*, pp. 5, 9.

of Canterbury, was by his political genius and legal ability to be the main force in converting a constitution largely unwritten and vague, into one written and definite. In Magna Charta itself the liberty of the English church is assured in the first article, and a second guarantee for its freedom occupies the most prominent place in the enacting clause at the end of the document, — silent witness to its prominence in the national movement.

While the church of England since the Conquest had become more and more Romanized, more highly centralized, and more independent of royal control, — without, however, losing its national vigour, — the political government of England had been slowly changing from an absolute to a limited monarchy. Anglo-Saxon institutions of local self-government, depressed by the Conquest, had been revived in proportion as the king had found himself obliged to rely upon the support of the native English; the royal courts, under Henry II., had expanded into a kind of national assembly, and the very machinery of government by which the king exerted his power limited the facility of arbitrary action; cities had been granted charters, — notably London, which, if it did not play in England the commanding rôle of Paris in France, nevertheless, in the crises under John, Henry III., and even as late as the Wars of the Roses, gave always a temporary and sometimes a permanent advantage to its possessor; and finally, the new ministerial nobility of Henry I. and Henry II. had firmly established itself in the land. As the result of the Conqueror's separation of church and state had proved disastrous to the royal prerogative, so now the fruit of his separation of manors was fully ripe. Already in numerous rebellions the barons had been forced to combine with one another; they were now compelled to court the assistance of the native English.[1] The extent to which the constitution had developed may be partly measured by the fact that the rebellion against John was largely the work of the ministerial nobility, and that their objections to foreign service were couched in terms[2] which a modern lawyer would call "special pleading," and which plainly show the decay of feudal spirit. The language, no less than the terms of the Great Charter, is a valuable witness to the growth of the constitutional power of the baronage. Already — and Normandy only eleven years lost — a foreigner could scarcely appreciate, much less administer, the laws of England.[3]

Under Henry II. and Richard, the crown had overstrained its power; for this, as well as for his own misdeeds, John paid the penalty. At best, the Angevin system of administration had been the work of the deus ex machina; it lacked utterly that vitality and organic unity which only a constitution expressive of

---

[1] Freeman, Norm. Conq., IV., p. 71. Taswell-Langmead, Eng. Const. Hist., p. 58, n. 2.

[2] Walt. Cov., II., p. 217. Sel. Chart., pp. 277, 278. Dicentes se propter terras quas in Anglia tenent non debere regem extra regnum sequi nec ipsum euntum scutagio juvare. Cf. Rad. Cogges., p. 872; Sel. Chart., p. 277, and Stubbs' Const. Hist., I., p. 563, n. 3.

[3] *Vide* Matthew Paris, III., p. 252, and *infra*, p. 69.

popular life and crystallized custom can possess. It was too complete a system for the national incompleteness. The reigns of John and Henry III. cannot be logically separated; the great problem of each was the same. The growing nation had to grow into a national form of government, and the only government possible for a reviving Anglo-Saxon community was a free one. This made the reign of Henry III. an epitome of English history. A conflict, then, between the royal power and popular liberty was inevitable; John's conduct hastened it. Both sides sought to strengthen themselves by alliances, and in the character of these alliances as well as in the conduct of the struggle, the character of the reign of Henry III. was already foreshadowed.

Since John and Innocent had united in the consecration of Peter the Poitevin to the See of Winchester, they had been at variance till May 15, 1213. At that time in dire distress, John took a step which, while it left no permanent mark upon the English constitution, was of paramount importance throughout the reign of Henry III. Because he had offended God and Holy Church so deeply as to be greatly in need of the divine mercy, and because no other sign of repentance save the humiliation of himself and his kingdom was adequate to the occasion, — such is the tenor of the document,[1] — John, led by the inspiration of the Holy Ghost, not constrained by force nor driven by fear, but

---

[1] Rymer's Fœdera, I., pp. 111, 112. Sel. Chart., pp. 284-286.

through his own free-will and with the assent of the baronage of England, freely yields up his kingdom to Innocent and his Catholic successors, receiving it back as a fief and paying 1000 marks per annum as a token of perpetual obligation and concession. Peter's pence was to be paid as before, and liege homage to be performed[1] if John and the pope met. Had John lived long enough to be victor in the contest for absolute power, he would probably have proved as faithless to this oath as to all others, and it would have passed harmlessly away: as it was, he lived just long enough to welcome papal legates and to give the pope every opportunity to turn the parchment pledge into actual practice, and then died,— leaving a minor heir to take the same oath, to be burdened with the same tribute, to pass his life under the same ecclesiastical tutelage which formed his early character, and to allow the See of Rome through its legates to attain a height of power in England never equalled before or since. In the light of papal exactions throughout Henry's reign, and especially in connection with the Sicilian crown, the last words[2] of John's oath read like a mocking prophecy.

Eighteen months after John's surrender of England to the pope, the king was in worse plight than ever. Bouvines in France had been fought and lost, and in

---

[1] Actually performed to Nicholas of Tusculum, Ann. Wav., pp. 277, 278.

[2] Patrimonium b. Petri . . . . adjutor ero ad tenendum et defendendum contra omnes homines pro posse meo. Rymer, I., p. 112. Sel. Chart., p. 286.

England the barons, assembled at St. Edmund's, had openly threatened war.[1] Probably in order to break the force of the coalition against him, John issued, Nov. 21, 1214, his "Carta[2] ut liberæ sint electiones totius Angliæ." Since the days of Henry I. elections[3] had been canonical in form and free in theory; John's Charter converted theoretical freedom into actual. Whenever a vacancy occurred in bishopric or monastery, the chapter could now meet as soon as it wished and fill the vacancy by a free election. A royal license had first to be obtained, but this was not to be denied or deferred. If it should be — "quod absit" — the election was nevertheless to be held and the choice to be valid and binding. However desirable this ecclesiastical freedom might seem to the church, John's Charter not only failed to detach it from his enemies, but also during the reign of Henry III. established "a freedom of litigation and little more."[4] It opened the door for the pope a little wider, but to this Henry himself was apparently not disinclined.[5]

In spite of John's exertions, the day of Magna Charta arrived: Innocent had not been able to save him. The sole resource was a Bull of Dispensation[6]

---

[1] Mat. Par., II., p. 583.
[2] Sel. Chart., p. 288. Statutes of Realm, I., p. 5. Cf. Rymer, I., p. 126.
[3] For election of Roger of Salisbury, *vide* Sel. Chart., p. 288.
[4] Stubbs' Const. Hist., III., p. 315 and note.
[5] Cf. Mat. Par., III., pp. 169, 187.
[6] Rymer, I., pp. 135, 136. Cf. Pauli, Geschichte von England, III., p. 436.

and such further assistance in the way of diplomacy and excommunications as Rome's greatest pontiff could afford in such a crisis. The English church was paralyzed by the suspension of the great archbishop,[1] and for many a long year it remained under the domination of papal emissaries. The result of the struggle between John and Innocent, the powers of despotism on the one side, and the representatives of English freedom on the other, need not detain us. Ultimately young Henry was crowned, the Charters reconfirmed by the king and Gualo, Louis of France expelled, and under the healing policy of the great Earl Marshall and Gualo, wisest of papal legates, the realm was reduced to peace. But given the character of the young king, the character of his reign was already largely determined. Aliens were already in the land; John's Charter to the church was in full force; his oath of fealty to Rome had been renewed by Henry; the king was already a special object of papal regard and under papal influence; the Great Charter existed as the basic means for the preservation of national liberty; and the national church, baronage, and people, acting in unison, had achieved a triumph which — as an historical fact — doubled in a certain sense the value of the statute. Whatever the inadequacy of the Great Charter, as a rigid constitution for a growing nation, may have been, it certainly limited royal prerogative, guaranteed national rights, and furnished standing-

---

[1] Rymer, I., p. 139. Nov. 4, 1215.

ground for constitutional resistance to tyranny. As the winning of Magna Charta had been the first-fruits of English nationality, so in the evil days which followed the death of Stephen Langton the maintenance of its inviolability seemed to be the only pledge of continued national existence. As the administration of church and state fell more and more into the hands of aliens; as the folly and faithlessness of the king himself became more and more apparent; and as the peculiar character of governmental ills required the application of peculiar remedies, the "Struggle for the Charters" developed into a struggle for the principles which they implicitly contained, and for the logical extension of those principles as the sole guarantee for freedom and national existence. And so, in the course of time, the patriots of England raised the cry for the Provisions of Oxford as their fathers had done for the Great Charter, and their fathers' fathers for the laws of good king Edward. Although the chief importance of the Barons' War must always rest in its wonderful constitutional developments, yet to the men of the day the contest was not primarily a struggle for an ingenious political device, but to secure the right of native Englishmen to the enjoyment and fostering of their native heritage. The constitution was but a means to this end; the development of the constitution was necessarily based on Anglo-Saxon forces, and it naturally grew into the representative system. Through Magna Charta the barons had promised to the people their rights;

the Provisions of Oxford had given the barons power to fulfil their promise; but it was reserved for the genius of Simon de Montfort to accomplish its realization by placing the means for vindicating English liberty and nationality in the only hands qualified in the long run to achieve the task — those of the people themselves. A thorough investigation of the causes of the Barons' War — which are essentially the same as those of the Provisions of Oxford — can alone determine its true character in the widest scope with reference to the crown, the papacy, the English church and nation, and the constitution.

PART II

The Influence of the Friars

PROMINENT among the causes which awoke national instincts and won the Great Charter had been the loss of Normandy and the consequent exclusion of foreign interests. That English nationality deepened and broadened was largely due to an element of a very different kind, though itself of foreign origin. On the 11th of September,[1] 1224, a small body of men of unusual garb and appearance[2] landed at Dover. They were members of the order recently founded by Francis of Assisi and had been conveyed across the Channel by the charity of the monks of Fécamp.[3] Three of the nine, however, were of English birth. Following the track of the Dominicans who had preceded them three years before, they passed from Dover to Canterbury, thence to London and Oxford,[4] — part of their number remaining at each stopping-place. From such a humble beginning was destined to spring a movement which as "an instance of religious organization and propagandism is unexampled in the annals

---

[1] Thomas de Eccleston, De Adventu Frat. Min., p. 5.
[2] Chron. de Lanercost, p. 30. They were locked up as spies and thieves.
[3] Eccles., p. 7.
[4] Ibid., pp. 7, 9. Trivet's Annales sex regum Angliæ, p. 209.

of the world."[1] Within a little more than thirty years their numbers had increased one hundred and forty fold, and they counted forty-nine convents.[2] Among the membership many men of good birth and great influence came speedily to be included,[3] for the requirements for admission to the order were framed to that intent, rather than to attract the lower classes. The applicant must "beleve of the Catholyk feith; be suspecte of no erroure; be not bound to matrimony; be not unlawfully begotten; be hoole of body; be prompte of mynde; be not in det; be not a bonde man borne; be of good name and fame; be competently lernyd, or ellis that he be of such conditioun that he maye profete the bretherne by laboure and his reception maye be grete edification to the peple."[4] Yet these requirements by no means explain the firm hold which the order obtained upon England; this came from its adaptability to the needs of the time.

In view of the share which the national church had borne in winning the Charter, its political popularity had perhaps never been greater than in the early part of Henry's reign; its spiritual influence, however, was sadly to seek. It has been already mentioned that during the first century after the Conquest the church

---

[1] Brewer's Preface to Mon. Fran., p. xli.

[2] Eccles., p. 10. Dignum memoria quod secundo anno administrationis Fratris Petri, quinti ministri Angliæ, anno scilicet ab adventu fratrum in Angliam XXXII°, numerati sunt viventes fratres, in provincia Angliæ, in XLIX. locis, MCCXLII.

[3] Eccles., pp. 15-17. Multi probi baccalaurei et multi nobiles.

[4] Mon. Fran., App. VII., p. 574.

had become more and more Romanized, more and more hierarchical. As Rome herself through the acquirement of worldly power had lost, pari passu, her spiritual force, so also corruption and spiritual weakness had been engendered in England through contact with Rome and Roman methods. The biting sarcasm of Nigellus in his *Speculum Stultorum* shows how far degeneration from this source had gone by the time of Henry II. But farther than this, the Crusades had brought a Nemesis upon the church. The Saracens had not only not been Christianized but had actually paganized Christianity. Heretical ideas were imbibed from this source as well as from the study of Aristotle; strange thoughts, customs, even diseases, penetrated Europe from the East.[1] Naturally the towns, seats of commercial activity, were most affected by this movement. But precisely upon the towns, in England as elsewhere, the hold of the church was weakest. Not only had monks of early times chosen the country exclusively as their residence, but their claim to market rights and tolls had brought them into actual collision with many market-towns and boroughs.[2] A large and politically most important field of work was therefore almost wholly withdrawn from the action of the regular clergy, and either abandoned entirely or given over to the tender mercies of what was rapidly becoming a hereditary class of secular benefice-

---

[1] Mon. Fran., Pref., p. x.
[2] Pauli's Pictures of Old England. Otté's translation, Macmillan and Co., London, 1861, p. 44.

holders.[1] To complete the spiritual weakness of the church in England, the great secularizing conflict between pope and emperor was sustained, on the side of the former, largely by English resources. In regard to this struggle Matthew Paris writes[2] in 1239, "The reputation and authority of the pope have suffered disastrous loss; scandal has arisen and wise and holy men have begun greatly to fear for the honour of church, pope, and the whole body of the clergy."

Into this turmoil the Franciscans entered, throwing their whole heart and soul into their triple task of providing for the religious, physical, and mental welfare of the perishing population of the towns. They brought to the work their poverty, which made them one with the people, and even dependent[3] upon popular sympathy for their daily bread; their humility and devotion, which could hardly fail to win the hearts of those among whom they unweariedly laboured; their shrewd common sense and practical wisdom, such as befitted men thrown wholly upon their own mental resources in the quick reading of character, and deprived of the factitious aid of books.[4] Whether as preachers or

---

[1] Roberti Grosseteste Epistolæ, Ep. LII, pp. 159, 160. Mon. Fran., Pref., p. xiii.

[2] Mat. Par., III., 638. For the evil of the times, cf. Mon. Fran., Ep. Ad. xx., pp. 104, 105; Ep. xxxviii., p. 141. His diebus damnatissimis.

[3] Gifts to the friars in London varied from 6d. to 40s. Their smallness indicates the class from which they were received. Mon. Fran., pp. 493 *et seq.*; also Pref., pp. xli., xlii.

[4] St. Francis had answered a request for the ownership of a breviary, Ego breviarium, ego breviarium. Mon. Fran., Pref., p. xxxi. Green, I., p. 258.

teachers, their circumstances impelled them to base their appeals or instruction upon experience rather than on theory; the result could not be for a moment doubtful. What the monks and regular clergy had lost, these "missionaries to the towns" now won. Their unuttered philosophy of life struck even deeper root than their formal teaching. As the doctrines of Wycliffe undoubtedly fostered at a later date the socialistic tendencies inherent in the masses, so at this early period the thoroughly Christian democracy of the Mendicant Friars fostered the growth of the city commune,[1] which — in London especially — played such an important part in the Barons' War. It can scarcely be considered an accident that exactly in those towns in which the Friars had their firmest seats, the popular sentiment was most directly opposed to papal and royal tyranny, and in favour of reform in church and state. These two towns were London and Oxford.

In less than a month[2] after their landing, the Friars had reached the university-town and lost no time in letting their presence be felt.[3] Education played a no less important part in their general programme[4] than

---

[1] Ant. Leg., pp. 55, 61; Winton, p. 101; Wykes, p. 138.

[2] Landing Sept. 11, 1224, they left London for Oxford "ante festum Omnium Sanctorum," Eccles., p. 9.

[3] Eccles., pp. 17, 38. Et ita inundavit in provincia Anglicana donum sapientiæ ut ante absolutionem Fratris W. de Nothingham, essent in Anglia triginta lectores, qui solempniter disputabant, et tres vel quatuor, qui sine disputatione legebant.

[4] In 1225 their first warden at London established a night-school. Factus est gardianus laicus quidam Lombardus, qui tunc primo de nocte didicit literas in ecclesia b. Petri de Cornhulle. Eccles., p. 10.

it did at a later day in Germany among the Brothers of the Common Life, and still later among the Jesuits, — and with an equally notable success. The remarkable poem [1] on the Battle of Lewes alone would prove how deeply the Friars pondered politics, if other signs were wanting. But they are not. It was in Oxford, in 1238, that the legate Otho, in full pontificals, fled into the church-tower for safety, while the students searched for him with angry shouts: [2] "Where is that usurer, simoniac, and plunderer of benefices, who thirsts after gold, perverts the king, subverts the realm, and enriches aliens from our spoils?" Not to mention other stormy scenes, there arose a great strife [3] in the University at the end of 1258 between scholars of different races, Scotch and Welsh, Northerners and Southerners, in which many beneath the rival banners were killed or wounded. A later historian sees in this the prelude to the later war and a justification of the ancient rhyme [4] —

> Chronica si penses cum pugnant Oxonienses,
> Post pancos menses volat ira per Angligenenses.

A surer proof, however, of the political leanings and

---

[1] Wright's Political Songs. Cf. Pauli, Tübinger Programm, pp. 28, 31.

[2] Mat. Par., Chron. Maj., III., p. 483. Ann. Mon. de Oseneia, pp. 84, 85.

[3] Mat. Par., V., pp. 726, 727.

[4] Wood, Hist. et Antiq. Univ. Oxon., I., p. 109. Certe bellum illud academicum in sequentibus regni tumultibus prælusisse, et antiquis hisce Rhythmis fidem fecisse videbatur, quoting MS. *Aurum ex Stercore* by Robert Talbot.

services of the Friars is seen in the mutual relations of the three great men to whom, more than to any others, the formation of a national-ecclesiastical party was due, — Adam of Marsh, a Minorite and the soul of the University of Oxford in his day ; Robert Grosseteste, the great bishop of Lincoln ; and Simon de Montfort.

In this movement Adam's importance is twofold : he is the intermediary between the University of Oxford and Grosseteste upon the one hand, and between Grosseteste and Leicester on the other. Of his two hundred and forty-seven letters preserved in the Monumenta Franciscana, one-third are addressed to these two men, sixty-two to Grosseteste. Such is the charm of the tender friendship which they reveal and so weighty is their information upon points of the greatest historical importance, that one is almost tempted to wish that *viva voce* intercourse had been curtailed, if so be the correspondence, voluminous as it is, could thereby have been increased.

The bishop of Lincoln was the Friars' staunchest friend. He desires to have them always with him,[1] enhances their influence by all means in his power, and defends them against their enemies. To the bishop of Lichfield he writes,[2] "We have heard that at Chester, in the presence of the people and some magnates, you bitterly abused the Minorites because they wished to live with the Dominicans there. This, if true, must have proceeded not from deliberation,

---

[1] Rob. Gross., Epist. XIV., XV., XX., XLI. Lanercost, p. 43.
[2] Rob. Gross., Epist. XXXIV., pp. 120–122.

but some sudden impulse. Your discretion knows how useful the presence and intercourse of the Friars Minors is to the people with whom they dwell, since both by the word of preaching and the example of a holy and heavenly conversation, and the devotion of continual prayer, they are indefatigable in promoting peace and in illuminating the country, and in this part supply in a great measure the defects of the prelates." Still more emphatically he adds, " Because, therefore, the conversation of the Minorites is the illumination of the people with whom they dwell to the understanding of the truth ; since it is in life a guide, stimulus, and attraction to peace, is no slight supplement to the defects of the prelates among whom they dwell, and is the occasion of abundance, not poverty, to others who are needy; no true lover of good can deliberately repel such a good, but must rather attract it with his whole strength." In these words we have the clue to Grosseteste's reasons for championing the Friars: through their religious zeal and usefulness he hoped to shame the secular clergy into purity and energy, to check the rising flood of infidelity, and to regenerate the land. In this programme the University of Oxford bore a leading part.

Without the efficient aid of Grosseteste, the Friars could scarcely have obtained a lodgment there, and he may have even summoned them himself ; at any rate, he became, in 1224, their first lecturer.[1] His interest

---

[1] Lanercost, p. 45. Gross. Ep., Pref., p. xxii. Eccles., p. 37. Sub quo inestimabiliter infra breve tempus, tam in concionibus quam prædicatione congruis subtilibus moralitatibus, profecerunt.

in the University never flagged thereafter. He plays the mediator in troubles between the students and the town, is active in the affair,[1] already mentioned, with the legate Otho, is consulted[2] by Adam in regard to the internal workings of the institution, and influences the character of the curriculum. Grosseteste had probably resided as chancellor[3] until 1235; meanwhile the Friars had been gaining possession of the chairs of theology in the University, largely through the efforts[4] of Adam of Marsh. That the bishop's sympathies were wholly enlisted on the side of this further development of theological studies, is shown by his remarkable letter[5] to the Regents of Theology. "Ye are builders of the house of God; the foundation-stones of his house are the Books of the Prophets — Moses among them; likewise the Books of the Apostles and Evangelists. There is a 'tempus fundandi' no less than a 'tempus ædificandi,' and that is the early morning hour." He seeks to model Oxford after Paris[6]

---

[1] For different versions, cf. Mat. Par., III., pp. 481–485. Dunst., p. 147. Burton, pp. 253, 254. Theok., p. 107.

[2] Adæ de Mar. Epist., Ep. XXII., p. 107.

[3] Wood, Hist. et Antiq. Univ. Oxon., II., p. 389. Pauli, Tübinger Programm, 1864, p. 12.

[4] Cf. Pauli, Tübinger Programm, pp. 20, 21. Bei solchen und ähnlichen Anlässen hauptsächlich scheint es gelungen zu sein den Minoriten ein in der That unvergleichliches Vorrecht zu erobern, das wesentlich zu ihrer Herrschaft an der Universität beigetragen hat.

[5] Rob. Gross., Epist. CXXIII., pp. 346, 347. Written *circa* 1240 or 1246.

[6] Rob. Gross., Epist. CXXIII., p. 347. Wood, Hist. I., p. 94. Innocentius . . . Episcopo Lincoln. Nos tuis supplicationibus inclinati, præsentium tibi auctoritate concedimus, ut nullum ibi docere in

and with brilliant success.[1] The foundation of the University jurisdiction[2] was probably laid by his jealous care, and as a last mark of his affection he bequeathed[3] his books to the Convent of the Oxford Minorites. The permanence of his influence is attested no less by the Oxford students' firm support[4] of de Montfort in the Barons' War, than by the formal statement[5] of the University in 1307 when it joined with Edward I. in the endeavour to enroll the great bishop's name in the calendar of saints. "Never was he known to abandon any good work pertaining to his office or his duty through fear of any man, but was ever ready for martyrdom if the sword of the smiter should smite him." When we consider that Oxford probably counted thirty thousand[6] students in these latter days, and weigh the political as well as the religious importance of the city in the troubles of the realm, we must assuredly rank Grosseteste's Oxford efforts high among the causes which made for the growth of English national sentiments and freedom.

It must not be supposed that Grosseteste's connec-

---

aliqua facultate permittas, nisi qui secundum morem Parisiensem a te . . . examinatus fuerit.

[1] Rob. Gross., Epist. CXIV., p. 335. Mat. Par., V., p. 353. For Oxford's European reputation, *vide* Mon. Fran., Pref., p. lxxxi.

[2] Wood, Hist., I., p. 93, citing brief of May 10, 28 Hen. III.

[3] Trivet, Annales, p. 243.

[4] E.g., Chronicon Willielmi de Rishanger, p. 22. Walter de Hemingburgh, p. 311.

[5] Wood, Hist. et Antiq., I., p. 105. Rob. Gross. Epist., Pref., p. lxxxiv.

[6] Pauli, Tübinger Programm, p. 21, citing Huber, Eng. Univ. I., p. 117.

tion with Oxford and the Friars was formed with any avowed political purpose. Yet the religious and educational influence of the Friars and their whole system of independent thought could scarcely fail, when coupled with the political occurrences of the time, to bear political fruit. In their intimacy with Simon de Montfort, however, Grosseteste and Adam of Marsh were touching, more or less consciously, the very centre of political life and almost the sole hope of political freedom. It is certainly significant to find in the correspondence of Adam of Marsh an allusion to a treatise on tyranny[1] written by the head of the national-ecclesiastical party, sent to the Chancellor of the University of Oxford, and sealed with the seal of Simon de Montfort. The significance is doubled when in the same letter the statement occurs that Earl Simon is deeply[2] interested in Grosseteste's religious plans, and proposes, if possible, to organize a party for their realization. In addition, the zeal of the two friends for his general welfare, their sympathy for him in his troubles, exhortations to patience and long-suffering, advice as to his situation at court and how to improve it, together with actual help of the most important political kind,[3] attest their realization of his great value to the commonwealth. In a certain very true sense, de Montfort is their spiritual pupil,[4] and it can

---

[1] Ad. de Mar., Ep. XXV., pp. 110–112: "de principatu regni et tyrannidis."   [2] "Supra quam a multis credi posset."
[3] Ad. de Mar., Ep. CXLI., p. 270.
[4] Cf. Rish. Chronica, p. 36, cited *infra*, p. 30, n. 1. Mat. Par., V.,

scarcely be doubted that the popular enthusiasm for the earl as the great champion of religious freedom was largely founded on his intimacy with Grosseteste. It is a touching, but unconscious, tribute, which one chronicler pays to both by closing the roll of the dead leader's virtues with the fact of this friendship.[1] There is a legend which testifies still more strikingly to their juxtaposition in the popular mind.[2] Just before the battle of Evesham a youth was brought to be healed at Grosseteste's tomb. He fell asleep, and on waking said that the holy bishop had gone to Evesham to the assistance of de Montfort, who was about to die there. It was even said[3] that Grosseteste had foretold earl Simon's death : "Laying his hand on the head of the earl's eldest son, he said to him, O fili carissime ! et tu et pater tuus ambo moriemini uno die, unoque die et morbo, pro justitia." As de Montfort's success was dependent on his popularity and moral worth, this reputation was invaluable to him ; while, conversely, his association with Grosseteste and the Friars enabled him to understand the working of the popular mind,

---

pp. 415, 416. Lincolniensis, cui comes tanquam patri confessori extitit familiarissimus.

[1] Rish. Chronica, p. 36. Beato Roberto . . . adhærere (comes Legrecestriæ) satagebat, eique suos parvulos tradidit nutriendos. Ipsius concilio tractabat ardua, tentabat dubia, finivit inchoata, ea maxime per quæ meritum sibi succrescere æstimabat. Cf. Rish. Chronicon, p. 7. Ad. de Mar., Ep. XXV., p. 110, etc.

[2] Rish. Chronicon, p. 71, among the Miracula Simonis. Cited by Luard in this connection, Rob. Gross. Epist., Pref., p. lxxxvi, n. 3.

[3] Rish. Chronicon, p. 7. For variation in wording, *vide* Rish. Chronica, p. 36.

to sympathize with popular objects, and ultimately to incorporate the people in his general plan of government. There exists apparently no other reason for Simon's superiority to the rest of the English baronage in the breadth and democratic character of his views, than his deeper piety and constant intimacy with the Minorites and their supporters.

The history of the many abortive attempts during Grosseteste's life to control royal misgovernment had shown clearly — and events after the meeting of the parliament of Oxford were to show still more conclusively — that the baronage as a secular power, influenced by selfish aims and torn by discord, was unable, single-handed, to solve the problem. It was the misfortune of the church to lie at the mercy of king and pope, who usually combined their powers for extortion. Even when the royal caprice resisted papal exactions, the clergy dared not lean for support on such a shaking reed.[1] The church, moreover, had been fatally weakened by the intrusion of foreigners into its highest offices and by excessive taxation; and the baronage had viewed its struggles with indifference until it was discovered that, in proportion as the clergy were impoverished, the national burdens pressed with additional force upon the laity.[2] In these circumstances Grosseteste did all that man could do. He resisted

---

[1] Mat. Par., IV., p. 559. Multi itaque prælatorum, timentes regis in hoc suo concepto proposito instabilitatem et consilii regii pusillanimitatem, partem papalem confovebant (1246).
[2] Lingard, Hist. of England, III., p. 115.

papal tyranny, rebuked royal extortion and the misgovernment of both church and realm, and in so far as was possible, encouraged an alliance between church and baronage. At the great reform parliament of 1244, the final word had lain with him. The king had produced a papal letter, and both by messengers and in person, had tried to induce the clergy to break their union with the baronage and grant him a separate aid. Grosseteste brought the discussion to a close by referring to the agreement with the barons, and uttering the prophetic words:[1] "We may not be divided from the common council, because it is written, 'If we are divided, we shall forthwith all die.'" His indirect influence through the Friars and the University of Oxford, as well as upon Leicester, has been already noticed. The result was, that although the time was not yet ripe for action, since oppression had not yet fused the elements of resistance into one, he had laid the foundations of a party which was to combine zeal for religious freedom with aspirations for national and political independence. His letter[2] to the Lords and Commons of the Realm and the Citizens of London is a trumpet-call to battle. It is an "appeal to the faithful children of the venerated English church in behalf of their fostering mother to restore her to her former state of peace, usefulness, and plenty." "The church is being worn out by constant oppressions; the pious

---

[1] Mat. Par., IV., pp. 362-366.
[2] Rob. Gross., Epist. CXXXI., pp. 442-444. Dated in 1252, according to Luard.

purposes of its early benefactors are being brought to nought by the confiscation of its ample patrimony to the uses of aliens, while the native English suffer. These aliens are not merely foreigners; they are the worst enemies[1] of England. They strive to tear the fleece and do not even know the faces of the sheep; they do not understand the English tongue, neglect the cure of souls, and impoverish the kingdom. Unless the speediest remedy is found, the church of England, anciently free, will be laden with a perpetual tribute through appeals to Rome and through the impositions, reservations, and provisions of the Apostolic See, whose claims, on account of the too great patience of Englishmen — nay, rather their folly — increase in extent from day to day. Therefore, let the noble Knighthood of England and the illustrious Commonalty of London and the Realm manfully rise to defend their fostering mother. Let them see to it, and know if it be fitting and expedient that the English be as sheep which bear fleeces, and oxen which carry yokes, not for themselves, but for others. That the realm of England may recover the pristine glory of its now tarnished name, that it may laudably perform its divine functions, and be strong to resist the spiritual enemies who cast their lustful eyes upon it, let the secular power be effectively armed to resist encroachments, and let the treasury be preserved for the sons of the soil. This will verily redound not merely to the unspeakable advan-

---

[1] Capitales inimici.

tage of the land itself and the perpetuation of its people's fame, but also to the glory of God." The year after this appeal was published, a noble victory seemed to have been won. With unusual solemnity the Great Charter was confirmed; fourteen bishops with bell, book, and candle excommunicated all infractors, and at the awful moment when the candles were extinguished and the words of the curse, "So may all who incur this judgment be extinguished and stink in hell" fell upon the startled air, the king exclaimed: "May God so help me as I shall faithfully maintain these things inviolate, as I am man, as I am Christian, as knight, and king crowned and anointed."[1] Grosseteste was one of the officiating bishops, but future woes seemed to oppress his prescient spirit, and one of his last public acts was to cause the Great Charter to be proclaimed throughout the length and breadth of his great diocese of Lincoln.[2] Upon his death-bed — if we may trust the great national chronicler[3] — his last words were a prophecy: "Nor will the church be freed from the bondage of Egypt, except at the point of the bloody sword; but these things now are light, yet in short space of time — within three years — heavier burdens are to come."

---

[1] Mat. Par., V., pp. 375–377. Rymer, I., pp. 289, 290. Burt, pp. 305, 306. Wav., p. 345. Liber de Ant. Leg., p. 18.

[2] Mat. Par., V., p. 378. Robertus præconizans in corde suo, et timens ne rex a pactis resiliret, fecit . . . excommunicare solempniter, in qualibet ecclesia parochia per diocesim suam, quæ præ numerositate sua vix possunt æstimare . . . infractores.

[3] Mat. Par., V., p. 407.

He had already[1] said that the Roman court, to work its wicked will, had made the king partaker in its crimes. The second statement explains the first, for the iniquities of pope and king had become so inextricably linked together, that both or neither must be assailed. Only with reference to this coming dual struggle can Grosseteste's prophecy and his life-work be correctly understood. Simon de Montfort, as at once the heir of Grosseteste's religious views and political sympathies,[2] and as the practical head of the English baronage, combined in his own person all the highest aspirations of the period, and inevitably became in the fulness of time the head of the national movement.

---

[1] Mat. Par., V., p. 407.

[2] Cf. Rish. Chronicon, p. 7. It was the preaching of the Friars after Evesham, and their use of Simon's life and deeds as a subject, which first revivified the national party. *Vide infra*, p. 198, 199, and n. 1.

CHAPTER II

THE FORCES WHICH ROUSED ENGLAND TO ARMED RESISTANCE

PART I

THE POETICAL LITERATURE

ADMIRERS of national songs and ballads have frequently ascribed to them marvellous power in shaping the destinies of nations, placing them in this respect above the laws. This on the broad scale may be true or false; to discover the exact influence of the songs of a particular period is the more important task, and it frequently baffles the historian. Thirteenth-century England is no exception to this rule: songs which mirrored the times existed in greater or less profusion, but the bare fact of existence is not infrequently the sole witness to their power. It is certain that they were composed by men whose interest in current events was deep, and that they afforded expression to popular opinion. Their subject-matter and the language in which they are written point unmistakably in most cases to the clergy as their authors, but there our knowledge ends.

In other instances, however, — and as good luck will have it, the most important ones, — the very fact of authorship determines the limit of their influence. Such capable critics [1] as Pauli and Green join in attributing the origin of the "remarkable Latin poems which treat of the leading ideas of the great popular movement and the sudden readiness of the third estate for a genuine constitutional form of government" to members of the order of St. Francis. The stimulative influence of the songs cannot in this case fall far short of the stimulative influence of their authors. The peculiar portability of the rhymed verses, and the close intimacy which existed between all members of the order, would ensure the wide transmission of the songs in their original form; the Friars' genius for preaching would transmute the ardent Latin into the more homely, but scarcely less glowing, native speech, while the general popularity of the Friars would guarantee them a vast audience. The more sublimated ideas might be lost in the process, but the substratum of hard sense would remain and be strengthened by practical applications such as the Friars best knew how to make. And upon the few choice spirits who could appreciate the depth and breadth and force of the original, the refined ideas would work with tenfold power. It is not too much to say that the strongest proof of the demand for the rise of the unrepresented

---

[1] Pauli, Bilder aus Alt-England, pp. 44, 45, from which the quotation *infra* is taken. Green, History of the English People, I., p. 265.

knighthood and commonalty to a share in the government of the realm — the writ to the parliament of Jan. 20, 1265, excepted — is the remarkable poem *On the Battle of Lewes*.[1] It is the only document which bases, or attempts to base, upon an adequate theory of government the great movement from which the reign of Henry III. derives its chief importance.

The songs of the reign of Henry III. are an especially valuable indication of the temper of the times. In the reign of John the eulogies and elegies which seem to have formed the bulk of the poetical literature in the early Anglo-Norman period had begun already to give way to the political satire.[2] Under Henry III. the movement goes rapidly on. The language changes from Latin to Anglo-Norman or a mixture of both,[3] until finally, when excitement has reached its height and the popular imagination mocks the conquered foe at Lewes, the first extant political poem in the English tongue appears.

> The Kyng of Alemaigne wende do ful wel,
> He saisede the mulne for a castel,

---

[1] A summary of this poem is given below, pp. 221-230.
[2] Wright's Pol. Songs, Pref., p. viii. Cf. p. 6.

> Savarics, reis cui cors sofraing
> Greu fara bon envasimen
> E pois a flac cor recrezen
> Jamais nuls hom en el non poing.

This song, though written by the younger Bertrand de Born, and therefore not English, is a fair sample of the early style, and applies to Henry even better than to John.

[3] Pol. Songs, pp. 51-56.

> With hare sharpe swerdes he grounde the stel,
> He wende that the sayles were mangonel
> To helpe Wyndesore.
> Richard, thah thou be ever trichard,
> Trichen shalt thou never more.[1]

The substance of the poems passes through three stages,[2] corresponding to certain great movements of the reign. The first stage turns from lament to complaint, from complaint to invective; the second demands reform and appeals to individual leaders; the third returns solemn thanks for victory and in impassioned language, but calmly perfect logic, seeks to justify the new basis of the state. But only too soon victory is changed to defeat, and the bursts of joy which hailed de Montfort conqueror and saviour die away into the accents of despair[3] or with deep religious feeling celebrate his martyrdom and enroll his name in the calendar of saints.

> Salve, Symon Montis-Fortis,
> Totius flos militiæ,
> Duras pœnas passus mortis,
> Protector gentis Angliæ.[4]

Without exception the songs of the whole period are on the popular side, a noble illustration of the position

---

[1] The whole poem is in Wright's Pol. Songs, pp. 69, 70. Wende = thought; trichard = deceiver.

[2] 1216-1258; 1258-1263; 1263-1272.

[3] Wright's Pol. Songs, pp. 125-127. Lament for Simon de Montfort, — "Més par sa mort, le cuens Mountfort conquist la victorie, Come ly martyr de Caunterbyr, finist sa vie."

[4] Pol. Songs, p. 124. Cf. for slightly different reading, Rish. Chronicon, pp. 109, 110, with addition of "Ora pro nobis, beati Symon ! ut digni efficiamur promissionibus Christi."

of the church and the national hero-worship of de Montfort. They touch upon purely secular abuses, but religious questions are their chief concern. They lament the lawlessness of the times and the growing infidelity;[1] they censure the avarice of Rome, where

> Munus et petitio currunt passu pari,
> Nummus eloquentia gaudet singulari.[2]

The debasement of the clergy as a spiritual body, the vitiation of the teachings of the church through the introduction of doctrines of expediency, and the consequent scorn of the clergy as entertained by the people are shown to be among the far-reaching results of universal venality.[3] The church falls, therefore, a helpless prey to the rapacity of pope and king, who unite their efforts to impoverish it.[4] "The king does not act wisely; living upon the robbery of Holy

---

[1] Pol. Songs, p. 47. Mundi status hodie multum variatur, Semper in deterius misere mutatur. . . . Rex et regni proceres satis sunt amari ; Omnes fere divites nimis sunt avari ; Pauper pauca possedens debet depilari, Et ut ditet divitem rebus spoliari. P. 48. Regnat nunc impietas, pietas fugatur ; Nobilisque largitas procul relegatur . . . Fidei perfidia jam parificatur.

[2] Cf. Pol. Songs, pp. 30, 31. Coram cardinalibus, coram patriarcha, Libra libros, reos res, Marcum vincit marca. To multiply examples is endless. P. 30. Roma, turpitudinis jacens in profundis, Virtutes præposterat opibus inmundis . . . *mutat quadrata rotundis.*

[3] Pol. Songs, p. 31. Roma cunctos erudit ut ad opus transvolent. P. 33. Non tam verbis inhiant quam famæ docentis.

[4] Pol. Songs, p. 43. Li rois ne l'apostoile ne pensent altrement, Mès coment au clers tolent lur or e lur argent. Co est tute la summe, Ke la pape de Rume Al rey trop consent, Pur aider sa curune La dime de clers li dune — De co en fet sun talent.

Church he knows he cannot thrive."[1] About seven years after these last lines were written, their corollary appeared; — Simon de Montfort is a tower of strength —

>Ce voir, et je m'acort
>Il eime dreit, et het le tort,
>Si avera la mestrie.[2]

The prophecy was speedily fulfilled at Lewes.

---

[1] Pol. Songs, p. 44.

[2] *Ibid.*, p. 61. Date is probably 1263. The preceding was evidently written during the Sicilian exactions.

PART II

THE ALIENATION OF LONDON FROM THE CROWN

EVEN in the days of William the Conqueror the city of London was of sufficient importance for him to think it wise to confirm its privileges by royal charter,[1] and since that time it had been steadily growing in political power and influence. One privilege after another had been accorded to it, until its position among the English cities had become unique. Even John, during the early years of his reign, had wooed it zealously and sought to beautify it.[2] The immediate result of his unwise change of policy had been the adhesion of the city to the barons, which in turn was followed by a great defection from the royal party; three weeks later John found himself compelled to sign the Magna Charta.[3] In this document London received additional proofs of its great importance: its mayor became one of the Charter's chosen guardians; it obtained the same privileges as the barons in the imposition of aids; and in common with other cities and towns it received the confirmation of its ancient liberties and customs.[4]

---

[1] Sel. Chart., pp. 82, 83.
[2] Pauli, Gesch. von Eng., III., p. 484.
[3] Stubbs' Const. Hist., I., p. 569. Cf. Pauli, Gesch. von Eng., III., p. 432.
[4] Sel. Chart., arts. 12, 13, pp. 298, 306. Stat. of Realm, I., p. 10. Rymer, I., p. 131.

With that shortsightedness, however, which was one of his characteristics, Henry III., disdaining the object-lesson which his father had received, not only refrained from conciliating the city but entered upon a course of action which bore him evil fruit in the days of the Barons' War. To rehearse the many indignities and injuries which he heaped upon the luckless city would be tedious. The pages of Matthew Paris and of the Book of the Ancient Laws [1] abound in instances. Nor is it necessary to trace the source of his behaviour; on one side, it was his chronic poverty, and on the other, his besetting vice of favouritism.

The latter led him to champion the cause of the Abbey of Westminster against the privileges of the city and incidentally to interfere seriously with the course of trade. Personal wrongs, such as Mayor Gerard Bat [2] had suffered, might be forgiven or passed over from fear, but by a certain transaction in the year 1248 Henry roused the lasting resentment of every tradesman in the city. It was his custom to celebrate the yearly feast of Edward the Confessor at Westminster; to make the occasion as magnificent as possible, and at the same time to favour his pet abbey, he established there a two weeks' fair. To ensure variety of merchandise and a large attendance, he

---

[1] Ant. Leg., pp. 8, 10, 14-16, 19-23, 25, 30-37, etc.
[2] Elected mayor in 1240. Henry refused to confirm him unless he would renounce the usual salary of £40. His pitiful reply to this demand — "Alas, my lord! out of this sum my daughter could have had a marriage portion" — so roused Henry's wrath that Bat was forced to resign altogether. Ant. Leg., p. 8. Mat. Par., IV., pp. 94, 95.

next decreed that at this time no other fairs should be held in England, and that on pain of forfeiture, no goods should be sold in London, whether under roof or in the open air. The throngs which came to Westminster answered the royal expectation, but the accommodations offered to the merchants were insufficient. The ground was muddy, and the wares, inadequately protected by mere canvas booths, were seriously injured.[1] Four years later a repetition of this process, under still more disadvantageous circumstances and with still more injurious results, roused the stings of memory and reawakened the ire of all.[2]

Midway between these two events, in the year 1250, there had occurred another breach between Westminster and London. Henry had endeavoured to force a deputation of the citizens to make important concessions to the abbot in exchange for certain privileges already theirs by right. They pleaded their inability to comply without the consent of the commune, whereupon the angry king suspended the action of the charter and took the administration of the city into his own hand.

The citizens then had recourse to Richard of Cornwall, Simon de Montfort, and other magnates of the council, with the result that these, fearing for their

---

[1] Mat. Par., V., pp. 28, 29. Ant. Leg., p. 14. This same affair damaged the fair of Ely. Mat. Par., V., pp. 29, 433.

[2] Mat. Par., V., pp. 333, 334. Nec pepercit eisdem propter hiemalis intemperiei inclementiam, lutum, pluviam, et loci ineptitudinem, quin tentoriis stare cogerentur. Exponere igitur jussit ipsis invitis merces suas, . . . non veritus omnium imprecationes, etc.

own immunities and vested rights, caused the decree to be annulled.[1] Here, apparently, begins Simon's friendly connection with this important factor in the later troubles of the reign; it was years afterward, when London and the barons were formally leagued for resistance, that this old suit between the city and Westminster was finally decided in favour of the former.[2] The happy coincidence could scarcely fail to strengthen Leicester's influence and power.

Although many examples of ill-treatment occur in the earlier part of his independent reign, yet Henry first seems to have adopted spoliation as a definite policy in the year 1248. Pecuniary aid having been positively refused by the July parliament of that year — on the ground of the impoverishment of the realm for aliens and the refusal of the king to appoint the three great officers of state [3] — Henry turned in despair to his foreign councillors, accused them of having brought him to this pass, and demanded their advice. It was resolved that he should sell his plate, "For," said the crafty aliens, "as all rivers flow back into the sea, so all those things which now are sold, will return to you as gifts." After the sale was over and the king had learned that London was the purchaser, he petulantly exclaimed: "Of a verity, if the treasure of

---

[1] Ant. Leg., pp. 15, 16. Mat. Par., V., pp. 127, 128. Regali autem voluntati, immo potius impetui et deliramento, restitit in quantum potuit major civitatis cum tota communa unanimiter.

[2] Ant. Leg., pp. 57, 58. In 1263.

[3] Mat. Par., V., pp. 20, 21.

Octavian[1] were up for sale, the city of London would absorb it all; these loutish Londoners are rich and call themselves 'barons' to the point of nausea; that city is an exhausted well of wealth." He forthwith conceived the plan of seizing frivolous pretexts for despoiling the citizens of their goods.[2] From this time on, the city was tallaged without mercy,[3] gifts were wrung from individual citizens, and the court, through the exaction of enormous prises, lived upon the plunder of the town.[4] The tide of misgovernment, which showed itself in the realm at large in the non-obstante clauses of papal bulls and continual violations of the Charters of Liberty, displayed itself in London by the violation of the city-charter and its frequent suspension for repurchase.[5] On at least one occasion, the dictates of a false policy led the monarch to construe as the payment of a customary debt[6] the gifts which the love of the citizens had been wont to give him on his return from a protracted absence; and his necessities drove

---

[1] *Vide* Mat. Par., IV., p. 624.

[2] Mat. Par., V., pp. 21, 22. The words "puteus inexhaustus" forcibly remind one of Innocent's speech at Lyons. Mat. Par., IV., pp. 546, 547. The policies in fact were identical, and led to similar results. For frivolous pretexts, *vide* (ex grege) Ant. Leg., p. 22. Mat. Par., V., p. 486.

[3] Ex grege, Mat. Par., V., pp. 101, 333, 568, 663. Rymer, I., p. 316.

[4] Ant. Leg., pp. 8, 16. Mat. Par., V., pp. 199, 485.

[5] Ant. Leg., pp. 19-22, 30-37, *et passim*.

[6] Mat. Par., V., pp. 485, 486. Et eidem adventanti centum libras, quod propter frequentiæ continuationem jam in debitam vertebat dom. rex consuetudinem, optulerunt, etc. . . . et sic xenium accepit, nec sereno, ut decuit, vultu acceptavit. Cf. V., p. 199. Non tanquam gratuita, sed jam quasi debita postulare.

him to exorbitant demands for presents which his insatiable greed prevented him from receiving with even a decent grace. Then, too, the pettiness of his nature caused him to inflict injuries which had not even the poor excuse of filling a temporary gap in the treasury, but which continued to sting and rankle long after they had passed out of the memory of their author. When, for instance, the king assumed the cross in solemn state at Westminster, in the year 1252, and but few of the citizens followed his example (for from long experience they scented this new device for getting money), he fell into a rage and called them baseborn money-grubbers.[1] An expression more offensive to high-spirited burghers would be hard to find. In the very year of the Mad Parliament, at a time when men were wont to gather in little knots at the street-corners, and when the most fantastic rumour became the basis for demands of vengeance, royal injustice brought Ralph Hardel, the mayor of the city, down with sorrow to the grave.[2] In the same year, while famine prevailed throughout all England and France;[3] while London was overcrowded with starving men and women fleeing from death in the

---

[1] Mat. Par., V., p. 282. Et objurgans vocavit Londonienses ignobiles mercenarios.

[2] Mat. Par., V., p. 675. Cives Londonienses, qui graviter de quibusdam enormitatibus coram rege accusabantur, redempti et multiformiter puniti, vex reconciliantur. Maximus autem eorum, sc. Radulphus Hardel, præ dolore obiit, qui major extitit. For the events which led to this, in which the king seems to have been guilty of the grossest chicanery, *vide* Ant. Leg., pp. 30–37.

[3] Fabyan's Chronicles, p. 343. Nangis, Chronique Latine, I., p. 219.

country-districts; while thousands were perishing in the city, and the rich were proclaiming by herald where bread might be obtained as a gift; when without the timely arrival of corn-ships sent from Germany by Richard, the king of the Romans, the people of the city must have perished from hunger;—at this time Henry attempted to seize the golden grain for his own use, and was forced by the law to surrender his plunder.[1]

During the anxious years between the parliament of Oxford and the end of the sharp campaign of 1263, when the citizens were being courted by the baronial party and the Commons were awaking to a sense of political power never enjoyed before, the citizens were dwelling beneath the shadow of a Tower which they rightly considered the stronghold of oppression,[2] and which, they knew, was fortified against them by means of their own wealth. At the very crisis of the struggle Prince Edward had craftily entered the New Temple, with iron hammers broken open the treasure-chests kept there, and carried off £1000 with which to pay his mercenary troops at Windsor.[3] Slight ground for wonder, then,

---

[1] Mat. Par., V., pp. 673, 674, 693, 694, 702, 710, 711, 728. Ant. Leg., p. 37. Fabyan, p. 341. Cf. Pauli, Gesch. von Eng., III., 714 and n. 4.

[2] Cf. Mat. Par., IV., pp. 93, 94. Erant (mœnia Turris) autem eis quasi spina in oculo. Audierant itaque minas objurgantium quod constructa erant memorata mœnia in eorum contumeliam, ut si quis eorum pro libertate civitatis certare præsumeret, ipsis recluderetur, vinculis mancipandus. (1241.)

[3] Dunst., p. 222.

that the Commons hailed the entrance of the barons with relief and joy, and that when the time for action came, fifteen thousand of the citizens sallied forth to battle for the right at Lewes.[1]

---

[1] Rish. Chronicon, p. 27.

PART III

THE ALIENATION OF SIMON DE MONTFORT FROM THE CROWN

ALTHOUGH as early as the 8th of April, 1230, Simon de Montfort had received a pension [1] of 400 marks per year until he should formally obtain the earldom of Leicester, he was undoubtedly classed by the men of the time with that swarm of aliens which descended upon England six years later on the occasion of the royal marriage. He was himself of foreign birth; at the queen's coronation he had carried the basin as High Steward of the realm; in 1238, with Henry's connivance, he had secretly married Eleanor, the king's sister, although she had previously taken a vow of chastity [2] and their children would be the heirs presumptive to the throne; and on departing for Rome to obtain Gregory's confirmation of his marriage, he had carried with him royal letters and a large sum of money extorted from the citizens of Leicester.[3] Among the English aristocracy he was fated never to outgrow completely what their jealousy con-

---

[1] Shirley, I., p. 362. For Simon's claim to the earldom, *vide* Pauli, Simon v. Montfort, pp. 20-30. Blaauw, The Barons' War, pp. 39, 40. Stubbs' Const. Hist., II., p. 55.

[2] Mat. Par., V., p. 235. Lanercost, p. 39. Trivet, p. 226.

[3] Mat. Par., III., pp. 338, 471, 479. The royal letters are translated by Blaauw, p. 43.

sidered the stigma of his foreign birth,[1] but his abilities and the vast services which he rendered his adopted country, together with his popular sympathies and love of justice, all conspired to place him in a commanding situation with the middle classes. It was reserved for Henry's folly to turn the man who might have been the brightest ornament of his court and the strongest supporter of his throne into an open enemy and the ultimate destroyer of the royal power.

De Montfort's early career in England is marked by strange alternations of favour and disfavour. On his return, in October, 1238, from his successful Roman journey, the king received him with a kiss,[2] and on the second of the following February gave him full investiture of the honour of Leicester.[3] Six months later Simon had been driven out of England by the monarch's insults. The occasion was as follows. Prince Edward had been born on the 16th of June, and the churching of the queen occurred in August.[4] When Simon and his wife presented themselves for participation in the ceremony, the king met them at the church-door with violent abuse. He shamelessly accused Simon of seduction before marriage, of obtaining the papal confirmation by corruption and then failing to pay the bribe, and of committing the unpardonable sin of presuming without authority to make the king his

---

[1] In 1265, Gloucester and others murmured, dicentes de Comite quod ridiculosum erat quod hic alienigena præsumabat, etc. Rish. Chronica, p. 32.   [2] Mat. Par., III., p. 498.
[3] *Ibid.*, p. 524. Theok., p. 111. Wav., p. 321.
[4] Mat. Par., III., pp. 539, 566. Quinto Idus Augusti.

surety. Having threatened him with excommunication, the king roughly forbade him to enter. In consternation and deepest grief, the earl returned to the palace of the bishop of Winchester, which the king had previously assigned to him as his residence, but a royal order speedily arrived for his expulsion.[1] Tears and prayers proving ineffectual, the earl, with his wife and following, fled across the channel.[2] The first breach[3] had now been made; never again could Simon regard his brother-in-law with feelings of affection or even personal respect, and he henceforth pursued an independent line of action.

His history for the next few years need not detain us. In April of 1240,[4] he came back to England and was received with honour by the fickle king. After his return from the crusade, he fought with bravery at Saintes, being "one of eight to win immortal glory" there, and in the following year he was one of the faithful few who remained with Henry at Bordeaux.[5] In the great movements of the next two years[6] he displayed his active sympathy with the reform-party, yet his favour with the king mounted steadily higher. The castle

---

[1] Mat. Par., III., pp. 566, 567.

[2] *Ibid.*, p. 567. Dunst., p. 151. Præ timore a facie regis fugientes.

[3] Pauli, Sim. v. Mont., pp. 36, 37, assigns the intrigues of the papal party as the cause of Henry's behaviour.

[4] Mat. Par., IV., p. 7.

[5] *Ibid.*, pp. 213, 231.

[6] In 1244, Simon was one of the twelve finance commissioners (Mat. Par., IV., p. 362), and in 1246 he was one of the signers of the baronial remonstrance to the pope. Burt., p. 283. Rymer, I., p. 265.

PART III   ALIENATION OF SIMON DE MONTFORT   53

of Kenilworth was placed in his keeping[1] and in the competition for the rich wardship of Gilbert de Umfranville he defeated Richard of Cornwall and gained an enemy for life.[2] It was not till 1248, that the king took the decisive, but unconscious,[3] step which led to the parting of the ways.

Gascony was the only land which England still retained upon the continent, and her retention of this country was due rather to her weakness than her strength. To the turbulent robber-barons of the south, the stern French rule was far from welcome; England's remoteness gave them a free hand. In Henry's need after the Poitevin war, they had simply sought to turn his weakness to their own advantage[4] and had been in a state of chronic rebellion ever since. Henry gladly availed himself of Simon's military genius and love of independence, made him viceroy of Gascony for six years, and instructed him to use harsh measures.[5]

Simon's success more than justified his appointment. In two campaigns he settled all questions with Navarre, captured the chief strongholds of the Gascon rebels, and sent Gaston de Béarn and other ringleaders to the king at Clarendon to throw themselves upon the royal mercy rather than upon his justice.[6] On the 30th of

---

[1] Rot. Pat., p. 28, Hen. III., Mem. 8.   [2] Mat. Par., IV., p. 415.
[3] Cf. Pauli, Gesch. von Eng., III., p. 681.
[4] Mat. Par., V., pp. 104, 208.
[5] *Ibid.*, p. 293. Cal. Rot. Pat., p. 22, Mem. 2. Ann. Hen. III., p. 32. For details of Gascony's condition, *vide* Pauli, Sim. v. Mont., pp. 51, 52.
[6] Rymer, I., p. 269. Mat. Par., V., pp. 103, 104.

November, 1249, Simon obtained Henry's acknowledgment: "We return hearty thanks to you for the care and enormous labour which you have expended so watchfully and manfully upon our affairs in Gascony, recognizing that your faithfulness and diligence yield no mediocre advantage to ourselves and our land of Gascony, and that they will also prove useful to our posterity forever and increase their honour."[1]

This fair sky was soon to cloud. The preceding letter had been penned by Henry before the prisoners reached Clarendon. On their arrival they were at once set at liberty, and Simon was informed[2] that they had sworn to keep the peace and were not to be molested. The work which he had accomplished under circumstances of exceptional difficulty[3] was in this way undone. But worse was to follow. In a letter written probably in April, 1249, Simon had told the king — "I have heard that they (the rebels) have given you to understand many sinister things of me; they will tell you soon that I was the cause of their rebellion."[4] In fact, from this time on, his Gascon enemies never ceased to intrigue against him, — with the result that the king became gradually alienated, failed to send supplies, and finally sought to disgrace him.

During a visit which Simon paid to England in Janu-

---

[1] Rymer, I., p. 271. Dated Clarendon. Pauli, Sim. v. Mont., p. 52, refers to this passage as if it had been written in the year 1248.

[2] Shirley, Royal Letters, II., pp. 56, 57. Dec. 28, 1249.

[3] For Simon's own account, *vide* Shirley, II., pp. 52, 53.

[4] *Ibid.*, p. 53.

ary, 1251, he received new light upon his situation. He came to ask the king for money and soldiers. The revenues of his own earldom of Leicester had already been exhausted, and the war could no longer be maintained without royal support. To spur Henry to action, Simon recapitulated the wrongs which the king himself had suffered in Gascony after the war of 1242, when the Gascons not only refrained from helping him but practised extortion,[1] and permitted him to lose both land and honour. "By the head of God, sir earl, you speak the truth, and since you fight for me so well, I will not refuse to give you aid enough. But there is an outcry against you, and grave charges are made. It is said that you imprison and plunder men who come to you in peace and also men whom you apparently summon in good faith." So spoke the king. The earl denied the truth of these accusations, adding that the king's own experience of Gascon treachery would adjudge them unworthy of credence. From his earldom and the wardship of Gilbert de Umfranville Simon raised a large sum of money; the duke of Brabant sent him troops; and so, with fresh hopes and a grant of 3000 marks from the treasury, he returned to his task,[2] now more arduous than ever. But even before his return to England in the autumn, he had again fallen from favour. In company with Guy of Lusignan he landed at Dover; the king came to meet them, greeted his half-brother

---

[1] Cf. Mat. Par., V., pp. 104, 105.
[2] *Ibid.*, pp. 208–210. Cf. Mon. Fran., Ep. Ad. de Mar., 146, p. 281.

cordially, and ordered London to be decorated in his honour. Leicester was ignored.[1]

Difficulties came to a head in 1252, when the secret insinuations of Simon's treason, avarice, extortion, cruelty, and general dishonesty had given place to open charges.[2] The king had already so far lent himself to these intrigues as to humiliate Simon publicly and to appoint a commission to investigate his conduct.[3] The rebels therefore felt sure of their ground. On the 6th of January Henry ordered the authorities at Bordeaux to send six representatives to lay complaints before him, and on the 1st of April, in accordance with a preconcerted plan, he sent letters-patent to the prelates, barons, and inhabitants of Gascony, summoning them to appear before him face to face with Simon.[4] Special safe-conducts[5] were also issued to Leicester's special enemies. On the 6th of March,[6] apparently after anxious consultations with the Gascons, the commission had made a report. Meanwhile the earl's English friends were active, and it was possibly through their influence that a second commission was appointed to traverse the judgment of the first.[7] Their report seems on the whole to have been favourable to Simon: "although he had treated some persons very harshly, they had received

---

[1] Mat. Par., V., p. 263. Ratione comitis fratris, non comitis Legrecestriæ, venit (rex) eis obviam lætabundus.

[2] Mat. Par., V., pp. 276, 287. Wykes, pp. 104, 105.

[3] Shirley, II., pp. 69, 76. Mat. Par., V., p. 277.

[4] Shirley, II., pp. 70, 71, 81, 83.

[5] *Ibid.*, p. 82.   [6] *Ibid.*, pp. 76–81.

[7] Mat. Par., V., pp. 288, 289.

no more than their deserts." Owing to Leicester's absence no full report was given at this time, although the archbishop of Bordeaux, the chief of the hostile deputation, loudly clamoured for it and for immediate judgment.[1] At length, in the earl's presence, the haughty prelate delivered his ultimatum: " The Gascons would never receive Simon as their ruler, nor obey him."[2] This reiterated assertion seems to have constituted the strength[3] of their argument, although from the 9th of May to nearly the middle of June they continued by night and by day, in secret and in public, to besiege the king's too willing ear with their mendacious complaints.[4] In the open sessions the nobility of the court rallied to Simon's support: Richard of Cornwall, because "the tribulation of the Gascons was well-pleasing in his sight;"[5] the earl of Gloucester and many other magnates, because they dreaded the national disgrace, if Henry — always favourable to foreigners — should impulsively order the earl to be seized and imprisoned; a few others, — among them the bishop of Worcester, Peter of Savoy, and Peter de Montfort, — apparently from love or principle.[6] It was only from this last class, according to the devoted Adam of Marsh, that the earl received efficient aid; yet the moral sup-

---

[1] Mat. Par., V., p. 289.
[2] Dunst., p. 184. Mat. Par., V., p. 289.
[3] Cf. Ep. Ad. de Mar., XXX., p. 126.
[4] *Ibid.*, p. 123. Quibus favor et audientia solempniter et private, non sine suggestionibus iniquitatis, jugiter sunt concessi.
[5] Mat. Par., V., p. 289. For reason *vide* V., pp. 291, 292, 294.
[6] Mat. Par., V., p. 289. Mon. Fran., Ep. Ad., XXX., p. 123.

port which was afforded by even the lip-service of the rest was of no slight assistance in curbing Henry's wilfulness.[1] During several days Simon bore unexampled abuse with unexampled patience; finally he obtained an opportunity to defend himself. He was prepared to employ either English or Gascon law,[2] and by his lucid reasoning, supplemented on every point by unimpeachable testimony, he utterly confuted his accusers. The commune[3] of Bordeaux sent under seal most striking witness in his favour; and much documentary evidence, still more weighty than personal testimony, was introduced, showing conclusively that the worst elements of the land were in conspiracy against Simon for checking their lawlessness.[4] On weighing the merits of the case the king himself was compelled to acknowledge de Montfort's innocence,[5] but although after this nothing remained to be done except to reward truth and punish falsehood, the stormy sessions still continued. The day following the king's acknowledgment, he broke out into renewed insults and rage,[6] as if determined on de Montfort's ruin by fair means or foul. It may have been the

---

[1] Mat. Par., V., p. 290.   [2] Dunst., p. 184.

[3] (Communitas) in qua quasi totum robur Vasconiæ ad distringendum hostiles et fideles protegendum, consistere dignoscitur. Ep. Ad., XXX., p. 124.

[4] *Ibid.*, p. 125.

[5] *Ibid.*, p. 127. Asserens illis condignam, istis vero nullum adhibendam esse credulitatem; hoc ipsum comite Richardo et cæteris tam prælatis ecclesiæ quam proceribus regni, quam et consiliariis clamantibus. In view of the discrepancies between Mat. Par. and Adam, the most probable version is obtained by combining both accounts.

[6] *Ibid.*, p. 127.

question of financial compensation which roused his anger; it may have been renewed intrigues. The earl recounted his services at Saintes; said that the king himself had persuaded him to go to Gascony and subdue the traitors there, that he had given him by charter the government for six years, but that he had not fulfilled his promise to give efficient aid.[1] Then he added:[2] "Lord king, you should firmly and truly keep your word. Either keep your bargain according to your charter, or pay back my expenses, for everybody knows that I have irreparably impoverished my earldom for your honour." Very unwisely the king rejoined, "I keep no contract with a traitor;. a covenant-maker need keep no faith with a covenant-breaker, but should rather destroy him." The impetuous earl could restrain his wrath no longer. He accused the king of telling a palpable lie and said it would go hard with him, were he not protected by the regal dignity and an empty title.[3] Had the magnates allowed it, Leicester would have been arrested on the spot. Their sympathy was on his side, however, and the earl continued: "Who could believe you were a Christian? Have you ever confessed? But what, after all, is confession without penitence and satisfaction? You may have confessed, but never yet were contrite or made reparation." After the king had furiously retorted, "Never have I so sincerely repented any deed as I now repent that I ever

---

[1] Mat. Par., V., pp. 290, 293. 10,000 marks.
[2] Mat. Par., V., p. 290. Cf. pp. 209, 210, 294.
[3] Mat. Par., V., p. 290. Nomine quoque umbratili.

allowed you to enter England or to have honours there," they were parted by their friends.[1]

For several days the long agony continued; Leicester sought to effect such a reconciliation as to ensure success in his government, but failing this, declared his intention to return at any rate and war the rebels down. With all the fondness of David for Uriah, Henry bade him by all means return "that he who loved war might have his fill and reap the reward of his father."[2] Four or five days later Simon landed at Bordeaux.

To a man of de Montfort's temperament and character the king's actions must have been peculiarly exasperating. He was himself the soul of honour, a lover of justice beyond all else, and especially tenacious in his purposes. Henry was his exact counterpart. A nagging persistency in wrong-doing seems to have been the most positive trait in his character, if we except the narrow piety, divorced from conduct, which made him fall an easy prey to Rome, and which lent de Montfort's words a keener sting. Never was Henry's wilfulness less serviceable to him than now. The effect of his conduct thus far had been to give Simon every reason for personal enmity and distrust, to enroll him among the creditors of the crown, to bring him into closer touch and sympathy with the hitherto-jealous baronage, and to remove him more and more in public

---

[1] Mat. Par., V., pp. 290, 291.
[2] Ep. Ad., XXX., pp. 127, 129. Mat. Par., V., p. 313. Cf. Dunst., p. 184. Simon's father was killed at Toulouse by a stone from a mangonel. Mat. Par., III., p. 57. Nangis, I., p. 191.

estimation from the ranks of the aliens.[1] The king had been in the wrong throughout.[2] To cap the climax, he now issued a series of edicts "so foolish," says Adam of Marsh,[3] "that unless divine power speedily interfere, they will redound to his own disherison, the weakening of the realm, disturbance of the people, and ruin of the earl." Doubtless it was for this last purpose that they were issued: they put de Montfort in the position of a criminal awaiting trial, forbade him to administer justice, finally deposed him from his office, and in general, inflicted worse insults upon him than have cost many a monarch his crown at the hands of an outraged subject.[4] After a hard campaign in which he fully maintained his military reputation, thinking that he was now justified in entrusting the land to the tender mercies of Henry and his youthful son, de Montfort bound the king to the payment of his debt, went to France, and there was offered the remarkable honour of the regency.[5] The prophet was evidently not without

---

[1] Cf. Mat. Par., V., pp. 338, 289. Comes Gloverniæ *in hoc casu* com. Simoni favorabilis. . . . Timebatur enim quamplurimum, ne rex per impetum festinum quia tam alienigenis propitius esse probatur, comitem virum *nobilem* et *naturalem* juberet capi.

[2] Mat. Par., V., pp. 291-294.

[3] Ep. Ad., XXX., p. 128.

[4] For the contents of these documents, *vide* Shirley, II., pp. 86-88, 90, 91. Rymer, I., pp. 282, 283. Wykes, p. 105. Mat. Par., V., p. 379. The attempt to ruin Simon appears most clearly in the command to audit his accounts and to report concerning Blanchefort Castle. Shirley, II., pp. 91, 92.

[5] Mat. Par., V., pp. 365, 371, 379. Shirley, II., pp. 68, 69, 384-386. Cf. Wykes, pp. 105, 106. Comes quidem L. animo saucius, odium quod ex amotione sua conceperat pro tempore dissimulando, in regno

honour in his native land at any rate, but to avoid the appearance of evil he declined the offer.

Gascony at once fell into the wildest confusion. Alfonso X. of Castile was induced to advance claims to the province; Gaston de Béarn and other restless spirits accepted him as their lord, and Bordeaux hastily summoned Henry to its aid lest all be lost.[1] The king's shame was the earl's honour and best justification. The danger from Castile was averted by Edward's marriage-treaty,[2] but Henry's incompetency furnished weapons to the Gascons,[3] and it was only after Simon's reappearance that the rebels were forced to submit. Imperious as his temper was, de Montfort was far from vindictive. Throughout the whole of his recent troubles Grosseteste and Adam of Marsh had been his faithful friends, comforters, and guides, and now he had graciously yielded to the solicitations of the former, forgiven Henry's hard words and crooked dealings, and appeared in the field at the head of a choice body of troops maintained at his own expense. The Gascons "feared him as they feared lightning," and the rising was soon quelled.[4]

From this time on, till 1258, Simon stood somewhat aloof from politics. His most decided action was the

---

Franciæ morabatur, expectans temporis opportunitatem, quo præmeditate calliditate, depositoribus suis solveret talionem.

[1] Mat. Par., V., pp. 365, 366, 370. Dunst., p. 188.

[2] Rymer, I., pp. 290, 296, 298, 300.

[3] Mat. Par., V., p. 410. Burt., p. 317.

[4] Mat. Par., V., pp. 415, 416. Mon. Fran., Ep. Ad., XXV., CXLIII., CXLVI., CI., et al.

speech in the Easter parliament of 1254 in which he unveiled the duplicity of the king's demand for money,[1] but during the following years he resided in France and devoted himself to his private affairs.[2] His litigation[3] with Henry for Eleanor's jointure does not seem to have interrupted their mutual toleration, for later de Montfort became a member of the French peace-commission,[4] and in 1257 he was one of four to be entrusted with the entire management of the Sicilian affair — with power to wind it up, if deemed advisable.[5]

After what had passed, however, the relations between Henry and Simon must have been simply those of toleration. The king feared Simon; Simon despised the king. The forces which had repelled him from the crown had attracted him to the side of the people. His relations with the barons had become more cordial, and his identification with Grosseteste's party more complete. Thanks to his own efforts and the wise counsels of his Franciscan friends,[6] the persecution which he had undergone had greatly strengthened his power to endure. In his Gascon government he had developed his military skill, and had already tasted the sweets, as well as the bitter, of assisting the poor against

---

[1] Mat. Par., V., p. 440.
[2] Shirley, II., pp. 107, 108.
[3] *Ibid.*, pp. 382, 303, 168-175, etc. Rymer, I., pp. 407, 446, etc. The dates range, including complications, from 1250 to September, 1264.
[4] Shirley, II., pp. 107, 108.
[5] Rymer, I., p. 359. June 28. Also erroneously under June, 1264.
[6] *Vide* Ep. Ad. de Mar., especially Nos. 22, 30, 34, 135, 137, 138, 141, 143, 146.

the rich, the small against the great;[1] and so, when misgovernment had reached its height in England, he was both willing and prepared to step out into a broader arena and to conduct a nobler fight for freedom.

---

[1] Shirley, II., p. 53. Simon to Henry. (Unsigned.) Et por ce que je sui si mauvoleu de les graunz genz de la terre, por ce que je sostien voz dreitures et de la poure genz contre aus, peril et honte me serait. . . .

PART IV

THE DENATIONALIZATION OF ENGLAND: THE STATE

It is a strange phenomenon in English history that the weakest of her kings should stand between the most obdurate and the ablest. Among all the fluctuations of Henry's time no element is by nature more changeable than he. Visionary, without the ability necessary to realize his dreams; narrowly pious, without the self-control essential to stability of character; extreme in his views of royal power, yet incapable alike of inspiring respect in his friends or fear in his foes — he must have drifted if left to himself. But he was not so left: from the very commencement of his reign he fell under influences which seized the salient points of his character and never relaxed their hold. Papal agents used his piety for their own ends, and the supple natives of Poitou and Provence employed his æstheticism and ideas of arbitrary power as a stepping-stone to greatness. Henry's policy, therefore, — in so far as he had a policy — is scarcely his own; it is rather the resultant of his personal character as acted upon by temporary advisers and chance circumstances than a well-considered plan of action. It was England's misfortune that Henry, from purely personal inclination, selected his counsellors from among the class most

F

dangerous to the welfare of the state. They encouraged his dreams of foreign greatness, fostered his ideas of arbitrary power, disparaged the wisdom of the native English, sought to drive them from the council-board, and in general committed Henry to a course of action diametrically opposite to the natural tendencies of the growing nation. He dropped the wise plan[1] of attaching the greatest English nobles to the crown, and at the same time withdrawing them from interests in foreign states, by marriage alliances with the royal house, and was drawn by the marriage of Isabella with Frederic II. into the hot-bed of continental politics. From the very first he cherished the idea of winning back from France the dominions[2] whose loss had been foremost among the causes which had made England, England, and it was not until the barons ruled the state that peace was finally ensured. His wars with France were three in number; in all alike he was the real aggressor, all were alike unpopular in England, all were mismanaged and failed disgracefully. In 1237 the magnates spoke of him as a king too "lightly led astray, who had never checked by arms or frightened off a single enemy of the realm, even the meanest; who had never increased the bounds of the kingdom, but rather straitened it and subjugated it for aliens."[3] Five years later the barons warned him

---

[1] Shirley, I., pp. 244-246.

[2] In 1223, at the death of Philip Augustus, he demanded Normandy. Mat. Par., III., p. 77. Dunst., p. 81. Rymer, I., p. 170.

[3] Mat. Par., III., p. 381.

against the war in which he lost Poitou: "Rich and illustrious kings, his predecessors, had possessed in France impregnable castles, ample lands, and mighty armies, yet they had neither been able to subdue the French nor even to keep what they already had; let him profit by their example."[1] To the voice of reason he was dumb. The cap-sheaf of his folly was the acceptance of the Sicilian crown. In a word, Henry's foreign policy was vicious because it was expensive, badly planned and worse executed, thoroughly unnational and reactionary, and through the introduction of aliens entailed lasting evils on the state.

The dislike of the English people for a standing army, manifested in modern times by the yearly passage of the Mutiny Act, and by that clause[2] of the Bill of Rights which states, "That the raising or keeping a standing army within the kingdom in time of peace, unless it be with consent of parliament, is against law," is of very ancient date. In one sense it finds expression in the clause[3] of Magna Charta which removed certain aliens from their bailiwicks, for in those far distant days every alien was, or might become, a mercenary. At any rate it was dangerous to allow the castles of the land to remain in their power. The first problem of the reign of Henry III., after his position on the throne was once established,

---

[1] Mat. Par., IV., p. 184.
[2] Sel. Chart., p. 524, art. 6.
[3] Sel. Chart., p. 302, clause 50. Stat. of Realm, I., p. 12. Rymer, I., p. 132.

was the expulsion of these aliens; it was solved by the overthrow[1] of Faukes de Breauté, in 1224, by Hubert de Burgh.

It seems strange that Henry in the face of the expressed wishes of the people, and despite the light of history, should persist in the reintroduction of a foreign element. Apart from papal influence and John's mercenary troops, he owed his crown, mainly, to the outburst of national feeling[2] which had deprived Louis of France of his supporters. A sound, though apparently ungrateful, policy had demanded the removal of John's mercenaries: it was also pledged by the Charter. The national life of England was growing stronger day by day when Henry, in default of recovering his foreign lands, began "to conquer England for them."

It was with much truth that de Burgh had said of Peter des Roches, that of all the evils which had happened in the days of John and Henry III., he had been the cause.[3] His appointment to the bishopric of Winchester by Innocent was an early example of the intrusion of a foreigner, and had enabled the pope to increase his power permanently.[4] He had been made justiciar by

---

[1] Mat. Par., III., pp. 87–89. Theok., p. 67.

[2] Mat. Par., II., p. 668. Cf. Mat. Par., III., p. 6. Dunst., p. 47. Quia vero Franci incipientes superbire, et nobiles Angliæ a suis consiliis elongare, cœperunt eos vocare proditores, et castra quæ ceperant sibi retinuerunt, et Anglis sua jura non restituerunt; ideo recesserunt ab eis comes Salesbyryæ, et W. junior Marescallus, et multi alii nobiles et potentes; et exinde de die in diem, pars Francorum cœpit deficere.

[3] Dunst., p. 84. In 1223.

[4] *Vide supra*, p. 8.

John for the express purposes of royal tyranny; his conduct had changed the wrath of the barons to fury, and was a signal warning against the introduction of aliens into the high offices of state.[1] His career under Henry III. is in all respects typical of the class which that king delighted to honour. He had all their disregard for the English constitution and ignorance of it. "There are no peers in England as in France; the king by his judges may proscribe and condemn any man in his realm," was the substance of his answer[2] when the king was accused of banishing men without the judgment of their peers. He exercised a baleful influence over Henry's mind, alienating him from English counsellors and encouraging his ideas of arbitrary power. By his intrigues the most faithful servant of the crown was removed from office and publicly disgraced, and his almost unparalleled services in the cause of English nationality were of no avail.[3] The same des Roches compassed the death of the Earl Marshall,[4] and thereby depriving the baronial party of their acknowledged head, threw England for a quarter of a century into a wild vortex of misgovernment. It was again des Roches who taught the king misgovernment as a science. Apparently at his suggestion Henry dismissed his native counsellors and instituted foreigners, complaisant and

---

[1] Waverley, p. 281. In 1214.
[2] Mat. Par., III., pp. 251, 252. Cf. Stubbs' Const. Hist., II., p. 49.
[3] Mat. Par. III., p. 220 et seq.
[4] Ibid., pp. 265, 266, 273–279, 288. Theok., pp. 92, 93. Dunst., pp. 136, 137.

of low degree.[1] The last and easy step to arbitrary rule was the dismissal of justiciar, chancellor, and treasurer, and the appointment in their stead of weak commissions, which would work the royal will. In this way Peter des Roches indirectly established the policy which gave the constitutional struggles of the reign their peculiar character. The readiest mode of curbing the king was the reappointment of the three great officers of state. Finally, from the same evil genius Henry learned the way to avoid performance of his public vows. There can scarcely be any doubt that it was the bishop of Winchester who privately procured that papal bull[2] which annulled the Charter and released the king from all his obligations, on the plea that ruled by evil counsels and misled by his youth, he had violated his coronation-oath by alienating rights which pertained to the crown. John set the precedent, Peter confirmed it, and Henry used it as a legitimate organ of government.

It was during the rule of Peter, in the year 1232, that the first of three swarms of aliens settled upon England. Poitevins and Bretons to the number of two thousand, eager for English gold, came at the call of their kin and were given congenial employment as guardians of castles and counties. Fat wardships and marriage-rights were entrusted to them, and posts in the

---

[1] Mat. Par., III., p. 240. Ut dicitur, de consilio Petri . . . omnes naturales curiæ suæ ministros suos a suis removit officiis, et Pictavenses extraneos . . . subrogavit. Et sic contigit ut illorum consilio . . . universa regni negotia ordinaret.

[2] Rymer, I., p. 229. June, 1236. Cf. Pauli, Gesch. von Eng., III., p. 594.

treasury. Abuses at once arose: bishop Peter thwarted the due course of law; and in the words of the chronicler,[1] "Judgment was entrusted to the oppressor, law to outlaws, peace to the quarrelsome, justice to the unjust." Time did its perfect work, and the magnitude of the abuses wrought their cure; for after the nobles had once risen in arms and Edmund of Canterbury had threatened the king with excommunication, the craven yielded and England was once more purged of the aliens.[2]

Although the clause,[3] "We will not make justices, constables, sheriffs, or bailiffs except from such as know the law of the land and mean to observe it," had been omitted from all of Henry's Charters, yet the people were insisting on its spirit and the consequent exclusion of foreigners from office. That hatred of aliens, which throughout Henry's reign steadily grew in intensity until it became a consuming fire, originated not in the bare fact of their foreign birth, but in their unconstitutional doctrines and utter lawlessness.[4] The two fundamental and essential questions of the reign — the maintenance of the Charters and of the exclusive right of the native English to rule in their own land —

[1] Mat. Par., III., pp. 240, 241.
[2] *Ibid.*, p. 245 *et seq.*, p. 272. Dunst., p. 136. Wykes, pp. 80, 81.
[3] Sel. Chart., p. 302, art. 45. Stat. of Realm, I., p. 11. Rymer, I., p. 132.
[4] In 1258, only those aliens were driven from England who refused to subscribe to the Provisions of Oxford, and who disobeyed them. Cf. Rish. Chronica, p. 3. Dunst., p. 222.

are strictly complementary and develop *pari passu*. Without the vantage-ground of Magna Charta, the aliens could not have been successfully resisted: if the resistance against the aliens had been unsuccessful, Magna Charta could not have survived. Freedom from continental interference had been the basis of all the distinctive points in the English constitution, and in the time of what may be termed the great Anglo-Saxon revival, when the government of the state was being organized and completed through the interlinking of central and local organs of administration, the interference of the most selfish continental elements could by no means be tolerated. As the struggle progressed, this truth became more and more apparent, until finally, just before the outbreak of the Barons' War, the exclusion of aliens from office became the central point of baronial policy, superseding even the Provisions of Oxford in importance, and giving tremendous weight to the national character of the movement.[1]

The present victory of the national party was of no long duration. Henry's marriage in 1237 gave the signal to a second swarm of aliens, the relatives of his wife; and ten years later, the death of his mother, who had married the traitorous Count de la Marche, served to introduce a third. Filial affection and conjugal love are excellent traits, but in Henry the defects of his qualities overshadowed the qualities themselves, and were displayed in nepotism and uxoriousness. For

---

[1] *Vide infra*, pp. 215–217.

twenty long years Henry, in sharp contrast to the king of France and Frederic II., allowed himself to be ruled by his wife's relatives and his own. All kinds of aliens, Poitevins and Provençals, Germans, and Italians, joined in the mad race for wealth and honours, and helped to swell the tide of general misgovernment. The national feeling which in Henry's reign had twice driven foreigners from England was by no means dead; but now no Hubert de Burgh was at the helm of state, and there was no great Earl Marshall to head an undivided baronage. Richard of Cornwall for a time maintained baronial rights, censured the king's misrule, even took up arms against him;[1] but he stood too near the crown, and the same year which saw the death of his wife, Isabella of Gloucester, witnessed his departure from the land on a crusade. His parting speech[2] to the prelates at Reading reveals his temper and the desire of his heart, but his policy was at variance with both: "Had I not assumed the cross, yet should I go, that I might not see the misfortune of my people and the devastation of a kingdom which I am believed to be able to protect, but cannot."

Isabella's death had snapped the last link which bound him to the English barons; his marriage in 1243 to Sancha of Provence, the sister of the queen, committed him irretrievably to the foreign party.[3] Henceforth his fall was rapid. His absence from the

---

[1] Mat. Par., III., pp. 411, 412, 475–479. Theok., p. 106. Shirley, II., p. 15.
[2] Mat. Par., IV., pp. 2, 11.   [3] Mat. Par., IV., pp. 2, 263.

parliament of 1249 — "quasi ex industria" — ruined bright hopes of obtaining the three great officers of state;[1] two years later he is classed among the aliens;[2] his election as king of the Romans placed his chief interests upon the continent; in 1258, the barons were glad to take advantage of his absence in order to carry out their plans of reform, and they dreaded his return as that of a disturbing element.[3] But in no case could Richard have played the part of a Simon de Montfort. It has already been shown[4] how the latter drew much of his strength from his connection with the deeply religious party founded by Grosseteste. With this element Richard had nothing in common except opposition to papal encroachments. In a letter[5] of May 18, 1257, on the occasion of a victory of his partisan, the archbishop of Mainz, over the archbishop of Treves, Richard writes exultingly to Edward: "Behold, what spirited and warlike prelates we have in Germany! It would be by no means disadvantageous to you, if such should be created in England, that by their aid you might be defended against the unseasonable attacks of your rebels." He evidently preferred a knightly Peter des Roches or a military boxer Boniface to the learned

---

[1] Mat. Par., V., p. 73.

[2] *Ibid.*, p. 229. Rex . . . spretis ac spoliatis Anglicis alienos introduxit; hinc com. Ricardum, hinc archiepiscopum, illinc Wintoniensem. . . .

[3] Wykes, pp. 118, 119, 121, 122. Rymer, I., p. 380. Burt., p. 461. Mat. Par., V., pp. 732-736. Shirley, II., pp. 132, 133. For Richard's policy, *vide* Stubbs' Const. Hist., II., pp. 61, 62.

[4] *Vide supra*, pp. 27-29.

[5] Rymer, I., p. 356. Burton, p. 394.

bishop of Lincoln or the saintly Oxonian Edmund. His denationalization was complete.

By the royal marriage England had been conquered for the natives of Provence and Savoy. The queen's uncles, William, the bishop-elect of Valence, Thomas of Flanders, Bernard, Boniface, and Peter of Savoy, had all entered England between 1236 and 1241 and had been given influential appointments in the state besides honours and gifts without number.[1] Nothing was for them too great or too small, from the archbishopric of Canterbury and the honour of Richmond to the custody of a castle or a yearly pension. Avarice and indifference to England's welfare were their distinguishing traits; the money which they received from the king or queen they were wont to use in the furtherance of their continental interests and then return for more. They were, however, by no means neglectful of their countrymen. Peter of Savoy, in particular, was empowered by letters-patent[2] to enlist in Henry's service as many foreigners as he saw fit, and their payment was practically left in his hands. A more potent engine for the denationalization of the realm would have been hard to find. The English, however, believed that it had been discovered when, in 1247, — the year when the Poitevins arrived — Thomas of Flanders imported[3] a bevy of foreign girls to be married to young English

---

[1] For details, *vide* Pauli, Gesch. von Eng., III., 626, 627. Blaauw, Barons' War, pp. 13-16, 18.
[2] Rymer, I., p. 242. June 23, 1241.
[3] Mat. Par., IV., pp. 598, 628. Cf. Rymer, I., p. 264.

nobles then in ward, and when Edmund of Lincoln and Richard de Burgh fell a prey to them. Men later came to think that a system of intermarriages formed the keystone of Henry's policy of arbitrary rule; by it he would debase the good old English blood and craftily entangle the leading members of the baronage in court-alliances of such a nature, that if the commonalty should dare to rise against the king and the aliens in defence of its rights, it would find itself impotent and destitute of leaders.[1] In particular, the marriage of the young and promising Gilbert of Gloucester to Alice of Angoulême had been felt as a heavy blow.[2] Henry had touched the nation in its tenderest point, the pride of blood, and it is in a tone of veiled rebellion that the great historian, in whose pages the England of the time is mirrored, sums up the strength of the two parties and foretells the coming of the storm.[3]

But bad as was the influence of the natives of Provence and hated as they were, yet bitterer by far was the advent of the Poitevins in 1247. No special harm had ever come to England from Provence, while the relations between England and Poitou had for the last thirty years consisted of tissue after tissue of treachery

---

[1] Mat. Par., V., p. 514. In 1255.
[2] Theok., p. 151. Mat. Par., V., p. 363. Anno quoque sub eodem (1253) indigenarum Angliæ argumentosus supplantator, volens omnes regni sui nobiles degenerare, ad sic totam Anglorum in eorum excidium propaginem annullare genealem atque eorundem sanguinem generosum melancolicis fæcibus alienorum perturbare, doluit quod saltem Ricardus comes Gloverniæ et ejus progenies ex fonte sulphureo non coinquinaretur. [3] Mat. Par., V., pp. 514, 515.

and falsehood. In the very centre of the web of intrigue had sat the Count de la Marche, the one to whom above all others the ultimate loss of Poitou had been due.[1] It was his children by Isabella, Henry's mother, who now came to claim the royal bounty. Henceforth the pages of the English chroniclers teem with the misdeeds of Guy and Geoffrey of Lusignan, Æthelmar, and William de Valence. They not only represented a third wave of invasion from the continent, and bore the burden of long-accumulating ills, but in themselves deserved their reputation. Their birth was much against them; their avarice surpassed that even of the Provençals. With the latter they speedily entered into such competition that the court was filled with the rivalries of "reginales" and "regales."[2] Their pride and their excesses were so great that inferiors could not live beneath them, nor their equals with them; they so trampled the people under foot that the "bitterest bitterness lay in the necessity for peace."[3] Their bailiffs played the part of thieves and plundered the people on all sides. The favourite answer of William de Bussey to complainants against him is said to have been, "If I do you wrong who shall do you right? The king wills whatever my lord, William de Valence, wills, but not *e converso*."[4] All

---

[1] Mat. Par., IV., p. 216. Theok., p. 124. Dunst., p. 158. Shirley, II., p. 28.
[2] Mat. Par., V., pp. 349–352.
[3] Rish., Chronicon, p. 5. Rymer, I., p. 373.
[4] Mat. Par., V., p. 738. Cf. Rish., Chronicon, pp. 4, 5. Chronica, p. 2.

the worst political abuses of the time centre round the names of these four brothers. Their influence over Henry was unbounded:[1] no one dared to complain against them to the king lest he should be not judge but adversary.[2] The days of the Heptarchy seemed to have returned, when England was ruled by a multitude of kings and anarchy prevailed.[3] To complete the general confusion, many even of the more illustrious English nobles seemed inclined to follow their example.[4]

Despite the popular ill-will, the king overwhelmed his brothers with favours. Guy and Geoffrey vibrated between England and the continent, departing loaded with gifts and returning empty for more.[5] William de Valence was knighted, admitted as a matter of course to the council-board, through the king's gift received Joanna, the heiress of Munchensey, as his wife, later obtained the wardship of the rich estates, and finally was graced with the lordship of Pembroke.[6] Æthelmar was given benefices extorted by the king from individ-

---

[1] Cf. Rymer, I., p. 373. Mat. Par., VI., pp. 403, 407.

[2] Rymer, I., p. 373. Cf. Mat. Par., V., p. 594. *Vide infra*, p. 153, n. 3.

[3] Mat. Par., V., pp. 229, 241, 316, 370, 494, 595. Taxster (apud Barthol. Cotton), p. 137. Theok., p. 175. Robert of Gloucester, p. 533. And the king hom let hor wille, that ech was as king, And nome pouere menne god, and ne paiede nothing. To eni of this bretheren zuf there pleinede eni wizt, Hii sede, zuf we doth ou wrong, wo ssal ou do rizt?

[4] Robert of Glouc., p. 533. Mat. Par., V., p. 316. Et sic facti sunt aliis deteriores.

[5] Mat. Par., IV., p. 650; V., pp. 205, 263.

[6] *Ibid.*, IV., pp. 627-629, 644, 650; V., p. 504. Ant. Leg., p. 12. Dunst., pp. 171, 172.

ual prelates, until he seemed richer than a bishop; and finally this stripling who, it was said, "had never submitted his hand to the ferule in the schools, who was ignorant of the rudiments of art and grammar, and did not understand the English speech or writing," was permitted to administer the rich bishopric of Winchester and draw its revenues. It was on this occasion that the grand cathedral witnessed the edifying spectacle of a king who, in the very act and article of violating canonical and chartered rights, preached to the monks upon the text, " Justice and Peace have kissed each other." [1]

To name at length the rank and file of these great armies of invasion, and to enumerate the infinite multiplicity of the gifts which they received would be alike tedious and fruitless. Henry was naturally fond of display and was lavish beyond the point of prodigality. Magnificent ceremonies, costly wars, demands from Rome, and gifts to aliens kept him chronically poor. As early as the year 1237, soon after the Provençals arrived, Richard of Cornwall had sharply rebuked the king for despoiling his nobles, impoverishing the kingdom, and imprudently enriching the insidious enemies of the realm. He added that Henry during his reign had collected enormous sums of money, had had the custody of every archbishopric and bishopric in England except three, had also had the incomes of abbacies, the wardship of baronies, and frequent escheats — and yet the treasury was empty.[2]

---

[1] Mat. Par., IV., 650; V., pp. 91, 179-184, 224, 227, 468.
[2] *Ibid.*, III., pp. 411, 477. Cf. IV., p. 186.

The amount of money spent was indeed enormous; but bitter as were the feelings of the plundered English solely on this account, they became tenfold bitterer when they saw the hated aliens rolling in wealth. As more foreigners arrived, the outgoes increased in proportion, and soon the national chronicler could write in anguish of soul, "Daily, no longer gradually, the king is losing the affection of his native people."[1]

The inevitable result of Henry's conduct was financial misgovernment and widespread discontent. The barons would not vote supplies to aliens or for unnational purposes: Henry dared not levy an aid without their consent. He was therefore driven to confirm the Charter in exchange for grants of money; but his faithlessness, and as some said, the counsel of the aliens,[2] led him to misapply the proceeds and, in full reliance upon papal aid, to disregard his oath.[3]

In default of grants, every expedient in taxation which extortionate selfishness could suggest and careless cruelty apply, was practised. London was systematically plundered; the Jews were so oppressed that in despair they asked to leave the realm;[4] the custody of vacant churches was a frequent source of lawless gain;[5] the crusades were used as a pretext; and the

---

[1] Mat. Par., V., p. 229. In 1251. [2] Mat. Par., V., pp. 378, 449.

[3] Taswell-Langmead, Eng. Const. Hist., p. 145, n. 2, mentions the number of confirmations of the charters in each reign through that of Henry VI.

[4] Mat. Par., V., pp. 441, 487. For extortions, *vide* Mat. Par., III., p. 543; IV., pp. 88, 260; V., pp. 114, 136, 274, etc.

[5] Ann. Burt., p. 420.

itinerant justices, seeming to recall the palmy days when Ralph Flambard drove his gemots to and fro throughout the kingdom,[1] proved ready instruments of extortion.[2] Prises and exactions through sheriffs and other royal bailiffs reached an unheard-of amount;[3] the king lived at free-quarters on abbots, priors, clerks, and men of even humbler station, and no entertainer was considered hospitable unless he gave splendid presents to the king, queen, Edward, and the royal train.[4] Money was made by selling rights of warren[5] in violation of the royal charters, and inquisitions into the state of the forests[6] produced on more than one occasion many thousand marks. Men were required to take up their knighthood, if possessed of fifteen librates of land.[7] The most casual means of obtaining revenue were used. In 1256 the king exacted heavy fines from all sheriffs who did not punctually pay their obligations to the treasury; and on the same occasion, every single sheriff in England was compelled to pay five marks for neglect of duty in not forcing all men of a certain degree of wealth to take up their knighthood.[8] Again, when the

---

[1] Cf. Stubbs' Const. Hist., I., p. 327.

[2] Mat. Par., IV., p. 34. The best proof of the exactions of justices, sheriffs, and bailiffs is found in the Petition of the Barons at Oxford (Sel. Chart., pp. 382–387. Burt., pp. 439–443), and kindred documents.

[3] Mat. Par., V., pp. 370, 371, *et passim*.

[4] *Ibid.*, p. 199.

[5] *Ibid.*, p. 356.

[6] *Ibid.*, IV., pp. 400,.401 ; V., pp. 136, 137.

[7] *Ibid.*, V., p. 560. Cf. p. 589. Ten.

[8] *Ibid.*, V., pp. 588, 589.

clipped coinage was called in and the new issue was made, — itself a process entailing heavy loss upon the people, — the king, by levying a heavy seigniorage and high exchange, used the opportunity to pay off his debt to Richard of Cornwall.[1] On days of festival or great occasions, money was sometimes given by individuals; if the present was small, the king showed no scruple in asking for more. At Edward's birth, particularly, messengers were sent throughout the land to announce the joyful news and to return with gifts: whence it became a current phrase in court-circles, "God gave this child to us, but the lord king has sold him."[2]

Rightly or wrongly, the chief share in these manifold wrong-doings was laid at the door of the aliens; at any rate, they ruled the treasury and seemed to feast when other men were fasting. That they favoured arbitrary government and were themselves lawless; that they were ignorant of the constitution, systematically disregarded[3] it, and incited the king to do the same, there could be no doubt. They supplemented in the state the great contemporary movement which was denationalizing the church, and lent the latter movement their support. Their avarice was so great that the woe prophesied by Joel as about to come upon Israel seemed to have fallen upon England: "That which

---

[1] Mat. Par., V., pp. 15, 18, 19, 629. Dunst., p. 175. Burton, p. 285. Osney, p. 97. Wykes, pp. 96, 97.

[2] Mat. Par., III., pp. 539, 540.

[3] Cf. Mat. Par., V., p. 316. Nihil curamus de lege regni. Quid ad nos de assisis, vel regni hujus consuetudinibus?

the palmer-worm hath left hath the locust eaten; and that which the locust hath left hath the canker-worm eaten; and that which the canker-worm hath left, hath the caterpillar eaten."[1] Their pride and contempt for the English was insupportable and ultimately received its due reward; for when the Poitevins opposed the national demand for constitutional reform, the universal discontent, long smothered, received adequate expression by their expulsion from the land.

---

[1] Joel i. 4. Cf. Ann. Burt., 464. The nuncio to the pope.

PART V

THE DENATIONALIZATION OF ENGLAND: THE CHURCH AND THE POPE

THE removal of aliens from the realm of England had been guaranteed by Magna Charta, but by a charter of a very different kind the power of one foreign potentate had been placed upon a basis in England more solid than before. The baleful influence of Peter des Roches had ultimately rendered the first provision nugatory; piety and policy, together with the king's well-grounded affection for Honorius III., conspired to make the second unassailable. And so it came to pass that while the state of England was being administered by aliens and in alien interests, a parallel denationalization was occurring in the church. One movement was the complement of the other, and each strengthened the other,[1] for their natures were essentially the same. The policy and conduct of the aliens from Poitou was the more frankly unnational and arbitrary at the start, and roused more speedily the jealousy and vengeance of the barons, while the material character of the aliens' power rendered them more open to attack; the hostility of Rome to England, more subtle in its character, more deadly in its effects, and less assailable on account of

---

[1] Cf. ex grege, Mat. Par., III., pp. 187, 241.

its spiritual nature and the indefiniteness of its power, was slower to develop, and roused the clergy to a comparatively hopeless resistance long before the baronage perceived their identity of interests and came to their help. The Poitevins favoured absolutism from habit and self-interest; the pope, from immemorial tradition and the very nature of his own power as the Vicar of Christ. It could scarcely be expected that the head of a strictly hierarchical church, which was seeking universal temporal sovereignty no less than spiritual, would favour aspirations for free institutions and for national separate existence — especially in the case of England, which by virtue of John's oath of fealty and its confirmation by Henry was considered a mere appanage of the Holy See.[1] Circumstances, however, delayed for a season the outward expression of this fundamental discord; the recall of Pandulf at Langton's instance, and the accompanying promise that no other legate should be appointed during the archbishop's life, averted a possible conflict between the overlordship of the pope and the national desire for self-government.[2] It was, therefore, not until the death-grapple between papacy and empire had fairly begun, that the ungloved hand of Rome was laid on England, and that the full effect of the inauspicious alliance between needy pope and arbitrary king was felt.

Meanwhile the kindly interest and wise counsels of Honorius were winning Henry's affection. "We re-

---

[1] Cf. Gardiner and Mullinger's Eng. Hist. for Students, pp. 70, 71.
[2] Dunst., p. 74. Green, Hist. of the Eng. People, I., pp. 267, 268.

joice," wrote [1] the pope, "to hear that your conduct is laudable in all respects, so that the flower of your youth seems to promise grateful and acceptable fruits; in this our joy is all the greater in proportion to our exceptional love and esteem for your person and realm. Since you are lord of a kingdom embracing many men and many minds, it is expedient that you be studiously kind and gracious to each and all, and that if controversies should unhappily arise, you should not become a partisan, but should correct, rule, and govern all sides with equal affection, equal diligence, and equal zeal: so that each party, recognizing your justice, may not fear to place their cause within your hands, but may trust you as a faithful vassal trusts his gracious lord, or a dutiful son his loving father." As the years rolled on, self-interest supplemented predilection, the papal influence deepened, and Henry's love for the person was transferred to the office as well. Even during the temporary breach of 1245, Henry signified his lasting attachment: "We intend to keep unimpaired, as we ought, all rights pertaining to our crown and kingly office, and desire the pope and the church to lend us their aid. You may be sure that we shall always exhibit and cherish utter obedience, faith, and devotion to the pope as to our spiritual father, and to the holy church of Rome as to our mother; in their adversity as in their prosperity we will adhere to them firmly, constantly, and loyally. . . . For beyond the general reasons which bind all Christian

---

Rymer, I., p. 177. March 14, 1225.

princes to the church, we are bound to her more closely than the rest for special reasons; when we were deprived of our father, while we were still in our nonage — regno nostro non solum a nobis averso sed et nobis adversante — mother Roman church herself, through the lord cardinal Gualo, then legate in England, recalled the realm to our peace and sway, consecrated and crowned us king, and seated us aloft upon the throne." [1]

Honorius doubtless meant to act for the best: his conduct, however, in the case of Faukes de Breauté, that "more than king in England," [2] shows but the more conclusively how grievously even the best-intentioned pope could err through ignorance of the actual conditions in the distant island.[3] Then, too, his indulgence and Henry's partiality to Rome were the chief causes of the heaviest grievances of the English church throughout the latter's reign.[4] As early as 1225 the expenses in connection with the papal court probably outweighed all other English outgoes;[5] in the following year, goaded by his need for money, the merciful Honorius himself made the first grand attack on patronage. Otho was sent as legate to demand for the pope's use two prebends in each cathedral and con-

---

[1] Ep. Rob. Gross., CXVII., pp. 338, 339. Grosseteste to Innocent IV., relating a conversation between himself and Henry.
[2] Theok., p. 64.
[3] Mat. Par., III., p. 105. Shirley, I., pp. 543-545, 547.
[4] Cf. Ep. Rob. Gross., Pref., p. xvi. Pauli, Gesch. von Eng., III., p. 566.
[5] Pauli, III., p. 566.

ventual church: his specious, but disgraceful, plea was the reduction of the expenses of litigation in the Roman curia and the abatement of notorious scandals which had arisen through Roman lust for gold.[1] This demand was refused, but Gregory IX. in his pontificate renewed[2] the attack frequently, and Innocent IV., by the use of non-obstante clauses, reduced the custom to a science.

The results of the intrusion of foreigners into English benefices are not far to seek. The realm at large was sadly impoverished by the constant drain of money; the lower clergy in particular were deprived of a career; the spirituality of the church was weakened and its unity of action paralyzed; through the infringement of the rights of noble patrons a reaction against the papal power was at this time occasioned, which tended to develop into a clamour for the secularization of the church estates;[3] the pope and king became so closely

---

[1] Dunst., p. 90. Mat. Par., III., pp. 98, 102, 103, 105 et seq. Osney, p. 67. Wykes, pp. 66, 67. Stubbs' Eng. Const. Hist., II., pp. 38, 39; III., pp. 320, 321.

[2] In 1231. Mat. Par., III., p. 208. In 1239 he endeavoured to extend the practice to livings in private patronage, but was defeated. Mat. Par., III., p. 610 et seq. In 1240 he ordered Canterbury, Salisbury, and Lincoln to provide for three hundred Romans. Mat. Par., IV., pp. 31, 32. For general summary, vide Stubbs' Const. Hist., II., pp. 38, 70; III., 320, 321.

[3] Cf. Rymer, I., p. 393. Burton, pp. 487–491. Alexander ad Magnates Angliæ, p. 490. Absit ergo, filii, ut propter appropriationes et provisiones hújusmodi ad revocationem et repetitionem juris patronatus quod vos dictosque prædecessores vestros præfatis religiosis asseritis concessisse, quomodolibet procedatis: cum non liceat vobis, quibus disponendi de rebus ecclesiasticis nulla prorsus est attributa facultas, extendere ad talia manus vestras, etc. (1259 or 1260.)

identified that one could scarcely be attacked apart from the other;[1] and finally an impetus was given to the great national movement of the reign — for not only were the barons roused to action, but the patriotic prelates and the lower clergy gave efficient aid. The cause of the national church and that of the reforming party in the state found here one connecting link.

The method by which intrusions were accomplished was no less exasperating than the practice itself. At York, for example, three strangers secretly entered the cathedral and asked a worshipper to point out the dean's stall. Then two of them said to the third as they placed him in the chair, " Brother, we install thee by the authority of the pope." Archbishop Sewall, a man renowned for holiness of life, tried later to invalidate this appointment and was suspended from his office for his pains.[2] The usurpation in this case was particularly glaring, but in very many instances an insult was added to an injury.

Honorius III. had instituted this pernicious custom; Gregory IX. extended and combined it with another politically worse. In 1229 came Stephen, demanding in the pope's name a tenth for the war against the emperor.[3] The clergy at first refused to make the grant, but a few days later yielded for fear of excom-

---

[1] Cf. Mat. Par., IV., pp. 10, 559, 561, 577, 655, *et passim;* V., p. 514.
[2] *Ibid.*, V., pp. 586, 624.
[3] *Ibid.*, III., pp. 186, 189, says that the tenth was demanded from clerks and laymen, and that the earl of Chester resisted. All other authorities refer it to the church alone.

munication, and the tenth was rigorously collected. Throughout the discussions the king sat silent, and by his silence seemed to give consent.[1] He had recently bound himself by his proctors at Rome to assent to this exaction in return for the cassation of Walter of Eynsham's election to the archbishopric of Canterbury and for the substitution of Richard, chancellor of Lincoln.[2] Here was the beginning of that shameful alliance which resulted in the degradation of the English church, and in such utter humiliation of the realm that a foreign potentate not only levied direct taxes in the land but was later allowed to collect them by his private agents. The king's explicit statement eleven years afterward, that he neither wished nor dared to thwart the pope in any matter,[3] scarcely required proof.

In the year 1231, Gregory ordered no presentments to be made to English livings till provision had been made for five Romans, names not stated.[4] In conjunction with Stephen's levying of tithes — so rigorous that it did not spare crops growing in the field [5] — this piece of papal insolence fanned all the fires of national enthusiasm. A secret society was formed whose members styled themselves the "universitas eorum qui magis volunt mori quam a Romanis confundi." They wrote threatening letters to the farmers of churches whose

---

[1] Mat. Par., III., pp. 186, 187. Burt., p. 245. Theok., p. 73. Dunst., p. 114. Wav., p. 305. Winton., p. 85. Wykes, p. 70. Osney, p. 70.
[2] Mat. Par., III., pp. 169, 170, 187. [4] *Ibid.*, III., p. 208.
[3] *Ibid.*, IV., p. 10. [5] *Ibid.*, pp. 188, 189.

revenues were due to Romans, forbidding them, on pain of personal injury and destruction of their property by fire, to send the revenues abroad; and they ordered all bishops, under like penalties, not to interfere with the chastisers of the Romans.[1] From threats they passed to deeds, seizing the persons of the foreign clerks, burning and pillaging.[2] This was by no means the work of a rabble, for Sir Robert Twenge, their leader, was the scion of a noble house of northern England, and when the royal bailiffs tried to seize some pillagers, the latter produced what purported to be letters-patent of the justiciar himself.[3] In all respects this movement, so early in the reign, is strongly analogous to the rising in 1263 which ushered in the Barons' War; and the politic measure by which the barons, in 1258, sought to attract the lower clergy to their standard may well have been suggested by the letters of those who preferred to die rather than be confounded by the Romans.[4]

In spite of opposition, the pope continued his exactions, the alien counsellors of the king gave him their support, and Henry was the ready instrument of both.

[1] Mat. Par., III., pp. 208–210.
[2] *Ibid.*, pp. 210, 211, 217. Dunst., pp. 128, 129.
[3] Mat. Par., III., pp. 217, 218. Dunst., p. 129.
[4] Cf. the passages in Mat. Par. and Rish. Chronicon. Par. III., p. 209. Pro certo scituri, quod si hujus mandati, quod absit extiteritis transgressores, quæ vestra sunt incendio subjacebunt, et pœnam, quam Romani incurrent in personis, vos . . . incurretis. Chron., p. 10. Adjungentes quod, si aliter facerent, sua incendio subjacerent, et nichilominus periculum quod Romanis imminebat in suis personis immineret. Rishanger had access to Matthew's writings.

"The fire of faith begins to cool," wrote Matthew Paris[1] in the year 1237; "charity has breathed its last, the liberty of the church is but a name, and religion is basely trodden under foot." But worse days were to come.

On the arrival of William de Valence in 1236, he had been made the king's principal councillor, to the great disgust of all the English magnates.[2] The January parliament of the following year had proved a stormy one. The king had received his coveted grant of a thirtieth, but only on condition[3] of the confirmation of the Charter, the removal of aliens from his council, and the appointment of four baronial nominees to administer the proceeds of the tax. In these circumstances Henry had recourse to papal aid, and at his request Otho was sent as legate to conciliate.[4] His moderation[5] won golden opinions for him for a time, but events were speedily to show that he brought not peace but a sword. During the three years[6] of his legation, by means of procurations, licenses for neglecting vows of crusade, usurpation of patronage, direct taxes, and by other agencies, he extorted a sum equal to full half the money in England, besides obtaining more than three hundred of the best prebends in the land for his own use or for

---

[1] Mat. Par., III., p. 389.

[2] *Ibid.*, p. 362. Dunst., pp. 145, 146. Theok., p. 102.

[3] Mat. Par., III., pp. 380-383; IV., p. 186. Rymer, I., p. 232. Theok., p. 105.

[4] Mat. Par., III., pp. 395, 403, 567.

[5] *Ibid.*, p. 403.

[6] June 29, 1237-January, 1241. Mat. Par., III., p. 395; IV., p. 84.

the pope's.¹ Except the king and Otho's beneficiaries, none grieved when he departed; his extravagant demands had cost the saintly Edmund of Canterbury his happiness and life, and had damaged the English church almost beyond repair.² Otho's coming coincided with that of the second swarm of aliens; it denationalized the church as these denationalized the state; it roused everywhere a storm of national indignation;³ and from this time dates the movement in the church which, supplementing the baronial agitations in the state, prepared the way for later armed resistance.⁴

With the accession of Innocent IV., Roman extortion began to reach the climax. With characteristic short-sightedness Henry had misused the lull before the storm — the vacancy in the papacy between Celestine IV. and Innocent — for a fruitless expedition to Gascony. Throughout the year 1243 royal exactions had consequently reached an almost unprecedented amount, and when Innocent's demand for aid against the emperor reached England in 1244, it found both baronage and clergy in a state of rage and desperation.⁵ The latter promptly sent a letter ⁶ of remonstrance and refusal: "As the Roman church has its own patrimony, whose administration pertains to the pope, so

---

[1] Mat. Par., III., pp. 567, 616; IV., pp. 6, 7, 9, 10, 15, 84. Burt., p. 257. Dunst., p. 154.
[2] Mat. Par., IV., p. 32. Winton., p. 88.
[3] *Vide* especially Mat. Par., III., pp. 481–485; IV., pp. 83, 84.
[4] Cf. Stubbs' Eng. Const. Hist., II., pp. 57, 58.
[5] Burt., p. 265. Cf. Mat. Par., IV., p. 39 *et seq.*
[6] Burt., p. 265. Mat. Par., IV., p. 39.

other churches have theirs, arising from bountiful grants of kings and princes. These are in no respect tributary to the pope or taxable by him: from these their patrimonies prelates should not be compelled to contribute." The king had already written [1] to the pope a general remonstrance against his exactions, and in the parliament of 1244 bishops and barons had united in a manner which seemed to promise better days.[2] The embassy of Martin, an envoy, not a legate but clothed with more than legatine authority, and of more than Roman arrogance,[3] seemed to join all three elements in an opposition to Rome which bade fair to be lasting. He suspended prelates from the collation of benefices until the pope's need was satisfied, demanded procurations from religious houses, collected all arrearages due since 1240, including the aid which Gregory IX. had claimed, and asked for a further grant of 10,000 marks.[4] In accordance with their own wishes and the order of the king, this was refused by the prelates, yet Martin succeeded in wringing large sums from individuals.[5] At length the barons took the matter up, and in the name of the "universitas regni" appointed Fulk Fitz Warin to send him out of England. Their emissary used but little ceremony:

---

[1] Mat. Par., IV., pp. 314, 315.

[2] *Ibid.*, pp. 362–366. *Vide supra*, p. 32.

[3] Mat. Par., IV., pp. 368, 379, 416, 443. Rymer, I., p. 262.

[4] Mat. Par., IV., pp. 284, 368, 369, 443. Rymer, I., p. 262. Dunst., pp. 166, 167.

[5] Mat. Par., IV., pp. 375, 379, 416, 443.

"If you will take advice, you will leave England before three days are up, that you and yours may not be hacked to pieces."[1] Martin appealed to the king for leave to remain, or at least for the grant of a safe-conduct, but received a still rougher reply.[2] At length, July 15, 1245, England was relieved of his hated presence.[3] The Council of Lyons had then been in session three weeks.[4]

Henry's own needs, the remonstrances of clergy and baronage, and the surpassing insolence of Martin's embassy and of papal demands, had emboldened the king to resist the papal tyranny. Envoys to the Council of Lyons had therefore been appointed. It was not their duty to join in the general glorification of the pope, but to present a declaration repudiating the further payment of John's tribute-money on the grounds that its exaction in time of war was injurious to England, and that "neither had their ancestors consented to its imposition nor would they themselves consent."[5] During the presentation the pope sat motionless and uttered not a word. The envoys next proceeded to read a letter[6] from the commonwealth (*universitas*) of England. It was couched in most courteous terms, but censured general legatine exactions, violations of the

---

[1] Mat. Par., IV., p. 420.
[2] Dunst., p. 167. Mat. Par., IV., pp. 420, 421. Diabolus te ad inferos inducat et perducat.
[3] Mat. Par., IV., p. 421. Cf. Dunst., p. 167.
[4] Mat. Par., IV., p. 431.
[5] *Ibid.*, pp., 419, 440, 479. Dunst., p. 168. Trivet, p. 234.
[6] Mat. Par., IV., pp. 441–444. Rymer, I., p. 262.

rights of private patrons, and the intrusion of aliens into English benefices to the detriment of spiritual interests, the impoverishment of the land, and the loss of the native English clergy. Martin's embassy received especial mention. After some days' delay [1] — ostensibly for purposes of consideration, — the envoys received an unsatisfactory reply. They left, protesting that from henceforth the revenues of at least those churches whose patronage was in the hands of nobles should never be extorted.[2] Before the council broke up, the pope gave a still more unequivocal proof of his intentions toward the English church and people by forcing the bishops present at Lyons to sign the very charter which the envoys of the realm had just repudiated.[3] The only fruit of the embassy had been a few paper-privileges: certain suspensions made by Martin were invalidated; only twelve benefices were reserved for papal appointees; bishops and other patrons were to be allowed the due exercise of their rights of presentation; and one Italian should never be allowed to immediately succeed another.[4] But no papal promise could restrain the operation of a non-obstante clause.

Never was a saying more indicative of settled policy

---

[1] Mat. Par., IV., pp. 444, 445. Trivet, p. 234.
[2] Mat. Par., IV., pp. 478, 479.
[3] *Ibid.*, p. 479.
[4] *Ibid.*, pp. 519, 520, 522. Rymer, I., pp. 262, 263. The immediate succession of Italians was a fruitful source of fraud. Before the English patron knew that the benefice was vacant through the death of the alien incumbent, another had been appointed.

than the celebrated speech of Innocent at this great
Council of Lyons: " Verily England is our garden of
delights; verily it is an unexhausted well; and where
many things abound, from the many can much be
extorted."[1] In addition to the general tax of a twentieth for three years levied upon the church universal,
England was favoured with a special demand[2] for a half,
a twentieth, and a third from different classes of the
clergy. The matter came up for discussion before a
special parliament convened at London, March 18, 1246.
Not only were these demands enormous, but in addition
the pope had failed to keep his former promises, meagre
as they were.[3] It was therefore decided that king,[4]
clergy, and baronage should each send a separate epistle
to the pope. The barons had now entered the contest
heart and soul; their letter[5] is a trumpet-call to battle.
The spiritual power of the pope is devoutly recognized,
to be sure, and he is greeted as the " chariot of Israel
and the horsemen thereof," but the threatening words
follow, — " Unless the king and the realm be very
speedily freed from their burdens, it will be incumbent
on us to establish a wall for the house of the Lord
and for the freedom of the kingdom." And again, —
" Unless these evils are very quickly corrected by you,

---

[1] Mat. Par., IV., pp. 546, 547.
[2] Ibid., p. 458. Burt., pp. 269, 276, 277.
[3] Mat. Par., IV., p. 519.
[4] Ibid., pp. 534–536. Rymer, I., p. 265. Dunst., pp. 169, 170.
[5] Mat. Par., IV., pp., 533, 534. Burt., pp. 283–285. Rymer, I.,
p. 265.

there is great reason to fear that such peril will threaten both the church of Rome and the king, that a remedy cannot be easily applied." Such words might hail the advent of a Wycliffe.

The six complaints which form the substance of the letter represent those peculiar evils of the church in England, which arose from Roman greed. Contrary to English law and custom, the pope was year by year extorting a heavier sum. Advowson-rights were violated, and Italian clerks, ignorant of the English tongue, were intruded into benefices to the imperilling of souls and the devastation of the kingdom. Papal pensions and provisions were a burden, nor did the pope observe the limits which he had himself established. Italian continued to succeed Italian, and contrary to English custom and the written indulgence [1] of former popes, Englishmen were forced to plead outside the realm. Without the consent of the king general taxes were levied and collected by the pope, the commonwealth protesting. "The land is burdened by the frequent arrival of that infamous envoy, non-obstante, by means of which the sanctity of oaths, ancient customs, force of documents, validity of concessions, statutes, laws, and privileges are weakened and pass away, while great numbers of Englishmen are heavily oppressed." [2] Finally, in the benefices of Italians, the ordinances of the bishops met with no observance; the poor were not supported, nor hospitality practised; the gospel was

---

[1] Rymer, I., p. 201. Theok., p. 75.
[2] Cf. Rob. Gross., Epist. CXXVIII., p. 434.

not preached, nor did souls receive due care; divine rites failed to be performed; churches were not adorned, and walls and roofs were falling to decay or were completely ruined. Such was the terrible indictment drawn by the barons of England against the secularized Roman church.

Their letter presented the theoretical and political side of the question; the clergy's was largely practical.[1] "The sum demanded was so great that it could not possibly be paid; England would be reduced to straits more dire than after the great tax which freed king Richard." They therefore appealed to a general council for relief.

Prominent among the causes for the king's attitude in this matter had been the discovery by actual computation in the year 1245, that the annual revenues drawn by Italian clerks from England amounted to upwards of 60,000 marks — a sum much greater than the clear income of the crown itself.[2] The king's anger had been still more recently excited by the papal concession to Boniface of Canterbury of the first fruits of his see for seven years, or until the sum should reach 10,000 marks.[3]

---

[1] Mat. Par., IV., pp. 531-533. Rymer, I., pp. 265, 266. Burt., pp. 278-282.

[2] Mat. Par., IV., p. 443. Rymer, I., p. 262. Cf. Mat. Par., V., p. 355 (1252). Episcopus R. Lincolniensis . . . fecit a suis clericis diligenter computari et considerari alienorum proventus in Anglia. . . . Reditusque clericorum per ipsum in Anglia alienorum, quos ecclesia Romana ditaverat, ad plus quam *septuaginta* milia marcarum ascendit. Redditus regis merus non ad ejus partem tertiam computatur. This may have been the same computation which Paris mentions.

[3] Mat. Par., IV., pp. 506-509.

Henry was therefore eager to oppose this new demand for tallage.

On the 1st of April, 1246, eight days before the envoys bearing the three letters of remonstrance left the island, the king issued a writ[1] forbidding the prelates to pay. At first sight, it seems strange that this command was disregarded, yet the very refusal of many of the clergy to obey the king throws a flood of light upon the circumstances of the time. In the greatest indignation Henry wrote[2] to the several bishops that he was in the highest degree surprised to find that they were acting contrary to the agreement in council to satisfy no papal demands until an answer had been received to the three remonstrances. Grosseteste responded:[3] "Rightly would you be surprised and indignant if, when bidden by the pope, we did not do a greater thing than this. For we see our spiritual father and mother forced to exile, straitened on all sides by persecutions and tribulations, despoiled of their own patrimony; and we are bound to honour, obey, revere, and help them in their necessities of every kind incomparably more than we are bound to do in the case of fleshly parents." In this reply, Grosseteste was traitor neither to his duty as foremost champion of the church against papal and royal abuses, nor to his settled principles. He simply fell a victim to the erroneous views of his day concerning the nature of the papal power. His view of

---

[1] Mat. Par., IV., pp. 551, 554.

[2] *Ibid.*, p. 558.

[3] Rob. Gross. Epist., CXIX., pp. 340-342.

church and state was the strictly orthodox view of the mediæval churchman. The object of each in its own sphere was to prepare the way to eternal blessedness, and their relations were complementary and mutually helpful.[1] The church, however, was the higher power, and therefore ought not to be entangled by the secular power in secular affairs.[2] In all things spiritual the pope must be obeyed so long as his commands were God's commands, otherwise they were to be resisted.[3] It followed as a corollary that papal demands upon the English church for money must be paid, if levied for lawful objects and in lawful ways. In the case at issue, the pope's decree was binding until formally revoked.[4] Grosseteste was the defender of the liberties of the English church against, first, *papal* violations of the canons and divine law, and second, *royal* violations of the rights of the church as both a chartered and privileged body. Because, however, the pope and king were as a rule so closely connected in their illegal exactions, and because the king could ultimately be constrained by force of arms only and by rebellion, Grosseteste foresaw the evil days[5] so close at hand and trained Simon

---

[1] Epist. CXXIV., p. 348. Est igitur . . . utrumque utriusque juvativum : ex quo evidenter sequitur quod neutrum neutrius est impeditivum.

[2] Epist. CXXIV., p. 349. Cum hoc esset solare lumen in lunare convertere, solares radios a vegetatione terræ nascentium præcludere, etc. Cf. Ann. Burt., p. 422.

[3] Epist. CXXVIII., pp. 432 *et seq.* The Lavagna letter.

[4] Epist. CXXIX., p. 341. Ad id compellit summi Pontificis auctoritas et præceptum, cui non obedire quasi peccatum est ariolandi et quasi scelus idololatriæ non adquiescere. I Sam. xv. 23.

[5] Cf. Mat. Par., V., p. 407.

de Montfort to be the champion of the church in the coming battle.

It is evident from the passage quoted above,[1] that the bishop of Lincoln's sympathies were enlisted on the side of the pope against the emperor, — partly as matter of duty, partly, perhaps, from horror at the latter's infidelity.[2] At any rate, scruples of this kind could not fail to weaken the position of the clergy in the year 1246; evils were so inextricably mingled with what the prelates considered a good, that the first entered the door with the second. Then, too, grave perils threatened the church from either side — from king as well as from pope. In these circumstances Henry's personal character had great weight. Because they distrusted his fickleness and the pusillanimity of the royal council, many prelates favoured Rome.[3]

On the 7th of July the clergy and magnates of the realm assembled at Winchester to receive the pope's final answer. It compared the king with the emperor, and ordered the prelates to satisfy the nuncio by the middle of August.[4] After a burst of impotent rage the king gave way, and 6000 marks left England to swell the coffers of the landgrave of Thüringia.[5]

Henry's spasmodic struggle had lasted two short years;

---

[1] Rob. Gross. Epist., CXIX., p. 341.

[2] Rob. Gross. Epist., Pref., p. xxviii.

[3] Mat. Par., IV., p. 559.

[4] *Ibid.*, pp. 561, 560. Rex Anglorum, qui jam recalcitrat et Fretherizat, suum habet consilium; ego vero meum habeo, quod et sequar.

[5] Mat. Par., IV., pp. 560, 561, 577.

its issue was universal despair and more intolerable servitude to Rome than formerly. In spite of paper-concessions[1] the rights of patrons continued to be violated; ecclesiastical penalties were employed to enforce the unrighteous demands of the pope; non-obstante clauses were introduced with even greater frequency; "avarice, simony, and usury flourished while true religion decayed." In truth, the case of England was peculiarly pitiable; she had surpassed all other nations in the vigour of her faith and of her devotion to Rome, but only to be trampled under foot by papal oppression and robbed of the fruits of her toil. A prey to every plunderer, she herself plundered none.[2]

Year by year, as royal misgovernment grew worse and worse, the alliance between the pope and king grew firmer. The latter needed help in enriching aliens from the revenues of the church,[3] and always looked upon a papal bull as the readiest means of relief from those troubles within the realm which were gradually assuming more threatening shape. The pope had even greater need of Henry and the wealth of England, for the struggle with the emperor was advancing apace and becoming a matter of life and death. The tenth for the crusade which was conceded[4] to Henry in 1250 by the

---

[1] Mat. Par., IV., p. 598; VI., pp. 260–264. Burt., pp. 314–317. Rymer, I., p. 294. Nov. 3, 1253.

[2] Mat. Par., V., p. 185. In 1250.

[3] *Vide* Mat. Par., V., pp. 224, 227, for bargain between king and pope: Æthelmar was to receive first fruits before confirmation; the son of the count of Burgundy, revenue of 500 marks.

[4] Rymer, I., p. 272.

pope offered a new opening for the extortions of both; while the king's acceptance of the Sicilian crown paved the way for exactions of hitherto unequalled ingenuity and magnitude. As the crown under Richard and John had overstrained its power through the over-elaboration of means of taxation and the extent of its use, so the pope now yielded to the same strong temptation, and ultimately paid a penalty still heavier. The struggles of the English people against the papal exactions which ensued upon the death of Stephen Langton, were the ground-swell which heralded the coming storm.

PART VI

THE DENATIONALIZATION OF ENGLAND: THE CHURCH AND THE KING

THE evils which Henry inflicted upon the English church flowed partly from his intimacy with Rome, partly from his fostering of aliens, partly from that chronic poverty which was caused by both these elements in conjunction with his visionary projects. The first led him to summon legates unwisely, and to allow papal taxation for non-national objects; the second caused improper presentations to bishoprics and benefices, and uncanonical interference with elections in violation of the Charters; the third led to a great variety of infringements of the rights of the church as both a chartered and privileged body. It is only fair to say that many grievances of the clergy based upon this last score arose from the innate antagonism between church and state, and must have been inflicted by any monarch who refused to tolerate an *imperium in imperio*. The extent of ecclesiastical jurisdiction over ecclesiastical persons, and the extent of the penalties which ecclesiastical courts could impose upon laymen guilty of spiritual offences, as well as the exact nature and limits of spiritual offences themselves, were questions as yet scarcely capable of definite statement and answer.[1] It remains true, nevertheless, that whether Henry in this last respect was intentionally guilty or not, he yet touched the sensibilities of the clergy in a very tender spot, and awoke the anger of a great corporate body which was especially jealous and tenacious of its peculiar privileges. Ecclesiastical immunities were in the eyes of churchmen a dogma of the highest rank, and around such citadels of faith conflicts are wont to rage with more than proverbial bitterness.

It is scarcely necessary to treat at greater length of Henry's alliance with the pope. Its ultimate tendencies were clearly seen as early as 1255, when Matthew Paris[2] wrote: "The pope is prepared and ready in all things to second the king's attempt to destroy the commonwealth of England, and will bind all royal opponents with the chains of anathema." One curious side-effect of the connection may, however, detain us for a moment.

On account of their ecclesiastical safeguards, the Great Charters were regarded as especially under the care of the clergy. The ecclesiastical documents corresponding to these Charters were the privileges guaranteed by papal bulls. It is scarcely possible, therefore, that the frequent violation of the latter by means of non-obstante clauses should not have influenced Henry in the non-observance of the Charters. He could not be his own dispensation, it is true, but the pope and

---

[1] They are best studied from the long lists of gravamina so common at this time, but require very special treatment.

[2] Mat. Par., V., p. 514.

the venal college of cardinals formed an *alter ego* admirable as he could wish. Certain it is that Henry was urged by his alien counsellors — who were practically identical with the Roman party at the court — to violate the Charters in reliance on the pope's assistance. A still more striking proof of the influence of the non-obstante in the same direction, was its introduction into civil courts in England to accomplish the cassation of royal letters-patent and of private charters.[1]

The introduction of aliens which denationalized the state by their charge of the royal counsels, the administration of the treasury and chancery, and the custody of royal castles to the danger of the land, is exactly paralleled by the denationalization of the church which resulted from their introduction to the care of the royal conscience, the administration of the finances of the church, and the possession of bishoprics and inferior ecclesiastical offices to the danger of souls. Then, too, as the cumulative effect of successive waves of invasion was felt in political spheres, so, also, in the sacred circle of the church.

The uncles of the queen had received a warm welcome from Henry and been given lucrative appointments in the state. To the great disturbance of the monks of Winchester he had caused their election of the noble Ralph Neville to be quashed by the pope, while in defiance of every canonical law and John's Charter he sought to intrude William of Valence.[2]

---

[1] Mat. Par., V., p. 210. Bishop of Carlyle *vs.* a certain baron.
[2] Mat. Par., III., pp. 489, 491, 493–495.

William's death prevented his success.[1] His former procurator, Peter of Aigueblanche, a Provençal, did not deserve, but met, a better fate. Through Henry's direct interference he was forced, despite his evil reputation and ignorance of English, into the bishopric of Hereford.[2] His whole influence was pernicious to the last degree, and with the possible exception of Æthelmar of Winchester, no other churchman was so hated.[3] It was the eminent misfortune of England at that day — whatever it may be in this — that every bishop was *per se* a force in politics. The efforts of this one were especially directed to furthering the interests of aliens, the king's arbitrary power, and abuses in the church. He was the agent for Richard's inauspicious marriage to Sancha,[4] he negotiated the Sicilian treaty,[5] and his extortions for the papal court were so shameless that through fear he rode out armed and guarded.[6]

It was reserved for Boniface of Savoy to win the richest prize of all. His election at the king's request as archbishop of Canterbury[7] was a national misfortune of the first magnitude. In times which demanded a Langton, the church received a head whose primary interests lay confessedly outside of England. Matthew Paris, writing in 1252, states[8] that Boniface had already

---

[1] Mat. Par., III., p. 623.

[2] *Ibid.*, IV., pp. 48, 74, 75; V., p. 422.

[3] Mat. Par., V., p. 510. Cujus memoria sulphureum fœtorem exhalat ac teterrimum.

[4] Mat. Par., IV., p. 190.

[5] Rymer, I., pp. 312, 316–318.

[6] Mat. Par., V., p. 591 (1256).

[7] *Ibid.*, IV., p. 104.

[8] *Ibid.*, V., p. 348.

drained the church and realm of 17,000 marks, had destroyed the forests in his see, and bestowed the richest revenues within his gift on aliens. His income had been used to aid his niece, Beatrice of Savoy, and the pope.[1] His sins of omission may have been worse than his sins of commission; but he who should have been a shield against hostile attacks was entangled in secular business, cared but little for his English flock, and passed his time abroad.[2] His active occupancy of the see of Canterbury, so far as it tended to good, was about equivalent to the occupancy of a Stephen Langton under a perpetual sentence of suspension.

The third swarm of aliens in the state was represented in the church by Æthelmar of Winchester. The mode of his election was utterly uncanonical, and his unfitness for the office was notorious.[3] Yet this youth acquired such influence over the mind of the king, that the barons, soon after his expulsion, wrote to the pope that Æthelmar's presence could overthrow in a moment all the reforms which they had instituted with untiring watchfulness and infinite toil.[4] The king, by great exertions, succeeded in obtaining for this brother permission to retain the first fruits of his see even before his consecration; soon after, another royal favourite, Laurence of St. Martin, bishop-elect of Roch-

---

[1] Mat. Par., IV., pp. 404, 405, 507 ; V., pp. 36, 37, 195.
[2] *Ibid.*, V., p. 515. Cf. Rymer, I., pp. 438, 444.
[3] Mat. Par., V., pp. 468, 224. *Non-obstantibus* juventute et literarum ignorantia et omnimoda ad tantam dignitatem et tot animarum regimen insufficientia.
[4] Mat. Par., VI., p. 403. Cf. p. 407. Rymer, I., p. 373

ester, received the same grace from the pope: thus by royal connivance and papal sanction it was ordained that "a bishop need not be a bishop, but only a bishop-elect; that the shepherd should not feed the sheep, but should himself be fed."[1]

The intrusion of foreigners into bishoprics, whether by canonical means or otherwise, was a blow of peculiar severity. Every bishop was a peer of the realm, and as such was entitled to a place in the council. His positive influence strengthened both papal and royal tyranny; his negative, weakened the resistant power of the church. The cleft in the councils of the baronage, which their own discords had occasioned, was caused in the case of the church by Henry's intrusion of aliens.

That "potestas cum petit, premit," is an ancient saying. By his prayers, which had practically all the force of law, the king intruded his nominees into the humbler offices of the church as well as into bishoprics.[2] The spiritual effect could not be doubtful; aliens unknown, who did not speak the English tongue, illiterate and thoroughly unworthy, careless of souls and greedy for money, outraged every sense of religious propriety. The king — it was well said — thought first of himself, of his nominee next, and of the people last of all.[3] No wonder

---

[1] Mat. Par., V., pp. 224, 241, 620, 621, 227. Ut scilicet pastor non pascat, sed pascatur.

[2] Mat. Par., V., p. 184. Patronatus oneri est jam, non honori; dampno, non utilitati.

[3] Burt., p. 423. Mat. Par., V., pp. 184, 329; VI., p. 354.

that the Minorites found a ready welcome; they were the heaven-sent antidote for the poison. The political effect was no less sure: a great body of eligible men of English birth, literate, discreet, and capable of doing good service, felt themselves defrauded of their rights, and helped to swell the ranks of those who sought to end the national disgrace.

The same poverty which led so directly to illegal exactions from the more helpless portions of the lay community was the fruitful source of violations of ecclesiastical rights. Men thought that there was no church of note in England from which, at one time or another, Henry had not extorted revenues.[1] A king who would not respect John's Charter of Liberties could scarcely be expected to observe John's Charter to the church. Of all Henry's oppressions, the misuse of ecclesiastical vacancies was perhaps the worst. Cathedral and conventual churches were tallaged and their lands left untilled; woods, parks, and fish-ponds were destroyed; buildings fell into decay; the villeins were impoverished and badly treated, and the church-estates so plundered that for some time succeeding prelates were forced to play the mendicant.[2] A considerable period usually elapsed before the impoverished church regained its former condition.[3]

---

[1] Mat. Par., V., pp. 184, 185, 362, 241. Nulla enim creditur fuisse notabilis ecclesia, de cujus uberibus in Anglia lac non creditur exsuxisse. Cf. III., p. 411; IV., p. 186.

[2] Burt., p. 423. Mat. Par., VI., p. 353.

[3] Cf. Mat. Par., V., p. 362. Dissipatis igitur bonis ecclesiæ vix poterant monachi (S. August. Cantuar.) per quinquennium respirare.

John's Charter had guaranteed a canonical election, and that with no delay. It was Henry's policy to interfere, and if his nominee were unsuccessful, he prolonged the vacancy and plundered the estates.[1] Perhaps the worst outrage of this kind occurred in the years 1256–1257 in the bishopric of Ely. On the principle "Ignotum tibi tu noli præponere notis," the monks refused to elect Henry de Wengham, the royal candidate, and chose Hugh Balsham, their prior, instead. The result was a contested election and one more appeal to Rome; the bishopric was frightfully devastated by the royal officials, while in the end the king was forced to submit and see the island pass under the control of an enemy of his own making.[2] It was not always that such poetical justice was meted out to him, for his chief objection to the prior's election had been that "the island of Ely from ancient times was wont to be a stronghold and camp of refuge for many men hard pressed in time of war; nor would it be safe to entrust the guardianship of such a place, strong as any castle, to any simple monk, unwarlike, feeble, and ignorant of the wisdom of the court."

It was in this same year — the year before the Mad Parliament of Oxford — that the convocation of the clergy submitted to the king a formal list[3] of their grievances against him; the number of the items was no less than fifty.

---

[1] Mat. Par., IV., p. 3.
[2] *Ibid.*, V., pp. 589, 619, 635, 652. Theok., p. 159. Dunst., p. 204.
[3] Mat. Par., V., p. 638; VI., pp. 353–365.

PART VII

THE SICILIAN CROWN

BARBAROSSA'S acquisition of the kingdom of the Two Sicilies through the marriage of Henry, his son, and Constance, the heiress of the Norman kings, was destined to be fatal to his house. The conflict for the headship of the world — originating largely in theoretical causes — had already been acquiring a character more and more territorial and local in proportion as the popes had advanced toward the realization of their dreams of temporal power. When Sicily and Lombardy had fairly become the two jaws of a vice whose function was to crush the papacy, this process was completed: sentence of death was passed upon the line of the Hohenstaufen when Alexander IV. announced[1] the fixed and perpetual policy of the See of Rome, — "Never shall the kingdom of Sicily be united and joined to the Empire."

At Frederic's deposition at the Council of Lyons,

---

[1] Rymer, I., p. 317 (1255). Cum nostra perpetua et firma voluntas existat ut numquam regnum Siciliæ uniatur vel jungatur imperio; videlicet, quod unus et idem et Romanorum Imperator et Siciliæ Rex existat. Cf., however, the utterance of Innocent IV. in 1253. Item regnum Imperio nullo modo subdetur, seu sibi unquam tempore in eadem persona aliquatenus unictur. Raynaldus, 1253, III. Mansi, T. II., XXI., p. 471.

I

Innocent had asserted his rights of suzerainty over the Sicilian kingdom as a fief which had been forfeited, and had announced his intention to dispose of it as he saw fit.[1] At the time of Frederic's death he continued the same policy, ordering the princes and imperial cities in Germany not to submit to Conrad's power, and writing to the Sicilian magnates that no Hohenstaufen was to be recognized as lord, for the sole lordship was vested in himself.[2] He also annulled such of Frederic's laws as were opposed to the laws of the church, and demanded full control of the administration of Italy, till he should appoint the emperor's successor.[3]

By Frederic's last will, Conrad had been made chief heir; in case of his death without male issue Henry, his brother, son of Isabella of England, was to succeed; and failing heirs to him, Manfred. The latter was created prince of Tarentum, and entrusted with the government of Sicily and the administration of all Italy during Conrad's absence.[4] Of all Frederic's sons Manfred was the ablest, truest, most proficient in the arts of ruling, and most beloved by the people. A strong party, however, had been formed against him by the intrigues of the pope, now in Italy, and he therefore lost no time in urging Conrad to appear in person. While awaiting his arrival, he entered perforce into

---

[1] Mat. Par., IV., pp. 454, 455. Cf. Wykes, p. 126.

[2] Raynaldus, 1251, III. Mansi, T. II., XXI., p. 436.

[3] Von Raumer, Gesch. der Hohenstaufen und ihrer Zeit, IV., pp. 175, 183.

[4] Mat. Par., V., p. 217. Burt., pp. 289, 290. Raynaldus, 1250, XXXIII. Mansi, T. II., XXI., p. 428.

negotiations with the pope, but the latter's proposals were not only unseasonable, exorbitant, and dishonourable, but were so long delayed that before they arrived hostilities had broken out.[1]

It was not until the 8th of January, 1252, that Conrad, after an unsuccessful campaign in Germany, entered his Apulian realm,[2] but once arrived, his progress was rapid. Before the end of the year, Manfred and he in brotherly union had won all the Sicilian kingdom, with the single exception of Naples.[3] The pope steadily refused to negotiate, treated Conrad as if deposed with Frederic, conducted himself as lord of the land, and diligently sought foreign aid.[4]

It was natural that he should turn to England first of all, for the struggle against the empire had long been sustained with English gold. As early as 1229 Gregory IX. had exacted[5] by direct taxation one-tenth of the property of the clergy, and in the year 1240 Frederick II., at that time Henry's brother-in-law, had found it necessary to write the king a letter of remonstrance, and to demand that the legate Otho be dismissed from England. The base answer was returned that Henry, of all princes in the world, was the most completely bound to obey the pope's commands, since he was the pope's sworn vassal and tributary.[6] From

---

[1] Von Raumer, IV., pp. 184, 186.
[2] *Ibid.*, pp. 178, 188.
[3] Naples fell Oct. 10, 1253. Von Raumer, IV., p. 190.
[4] *Ibid.*, IV., p. 188.
[5] Mat. Par., III., pp. 169, 186. Theok., p. 77.
[6] Mat. Par., IV., pp. 4, 5, 16–19.

a ruler so submissive, what might not Innocent expect?

In continuation of the same policy which in Frederic's lifetime had sought to raise up rival emperors,[1] — the landgrave of Thüringia, William of Holland, and Hacon of Norway,[2] — so the crown of Sicily had been offered already to Richard of Cornwall. According to Richard's own statement, this occurred at a dinner in Rome on the very day on which Louis IX. was captured at Damietta.[3] The offer was undoubtedly made on account of Richard's wealth, ambition, and relationship to Henry III.[4] The earl, however, was far too shrewd to accept an invitation which savoured so remarkably of that which once was made by another potentate on the top of an exceeding high mountain and in the words, "All these things will I give thee, if thou wilt fall down and worship me."[5]

Now, on the 3d of August, 1252, Innocent repeated the offer, on the specious plea that through Richard the world should have rest from its turmoil, and the church be tranquil and prosper.[6]

---

[1] Cf. Mat. Par., V., p. 201.

[2] Hacon's answer is memorable; it might have been made by Grosseteste: Se semper velle ecclesiæ inimicos, sed non omnes Papæ inimicos, impugnare. Mat. Par., V., p. 201.

[3] Mat. Par., V., pp. 111, 112, 347. April 5, 1250. Raynaldus, 1250, V. Mansi, T. II., XXI., p. 418.

[4] Mat. Par., V., p. 347. Noverat enim papa, quod comes hydropisi pecuniali insatiabiliter laborabat et dignitate temporali. V., p. 112. Sciens illum avidum et ambitiosum et multis thesauris abundare. V., p. 201. Quia vafer et abundans numismate et quia frater regis Angliæ.   [5] *Sic*, Mat. Par., V., p. 347.

[6] Rymer, I., p. 284. Innocent to Henry, urging him to use his

Richard had plenty of reasons for refusing — the state of his health, the danger involved in the subjugation of a realm so inaccessible from England, the dishonesty of supplanting Henry, his own nephew, and, above all, the fear of Roman intrigues and Apulian treachery.[1] His shrewdness and unwillingness to offend the pope led him, however, to reply that he would accept the offer, provided that all crusaders should be assigned to duty in Sicily; that the pope would pay half the expenses; give him certain cities and castles, together with hostages, as evidence of good faith, and would also secure him by written guarantees. "Otherwise," said he to Albert, the papal nuncio, "the pope might just as reasonably say, I sell you the moon at a bargain; just clamber up and take it." The answer of the pope was equally short and to the point: "With this man we care not to be leagued, or to have anything in common."[2] So ended the Cornwall episode. At a later day a sharp contrast did not fail to be drawn between Richard's wisdom and Henry's rash folly.

The pope had been treating meanwhile with different sons of France, and on the 12th of June, 1253, he definitely offered the crown to Charles of Anjou. It was refused on account of the harshness of the conditions, the absence of Louis from France, and general discon-

---

influence with Richard. For Henry's answer, promising an aid from the clergy, *vide* Rymer, I., p. 288. Jan. 28, 1253.

[1] Mat. Par., V., pp. 346, 347, 680. To these the influence of Conrad is added by Mat. Par., V., p. 361.

[2] Mat. Par., V., pp. 361, 457, 681.

tent with the project.¹ The pope's plan of marrying his nieces to Frederic's sons had also failed, and Innocent was therefore fain to console himself with the reflection that Henry would in no case have exerted himself so much for a nephew as he would for a son.² The crown of the Two Sicilies was accordingly offered to Henry for Edmund. To make the offer more tempting, Innocent promised that all crusaders should be diverted from the Holy Land to Sicily, — a promise whose fulfilment cost him nothing, — and added an indefinite assurance of further support.³ Henry had for some little time been nibbling at the bait and hesitating less on account of the enormous difficulty and expensiveness of the undertaking than on account of scruples against supplanting Henry his nephew. On the latter's death,⁴ he was finally induced to give consent.⁵ The concession⁶ was drawn up by Albert at Vêndome, March 6, 1254, and ten weeks later received Innocent's formal confirmation⁷ at Assisi. Comment is unnecessary. No definite terms were stated in the document, and on the very day on which he signed it Innocent

---

[1] Burt., p. 339. Raynaldus, 1253, II. Mansi, T. II., XXI., pp. 470, 471. Von Raumer, IV., p. 189.

[2] Mat. Par., V., pp. 274, 275, 301.

[3] *Ibid.*, pp. 457, 681. Cf. Rymer, I., p. 302.

[4] According to Von Raumer, IV., p. 193, Henry died December, 1253. According to Pauli, III., p. 695, "zu Ende 1253." Stubbs' Const. Hist., II., p. 71, dates "early in 1254." Cf. Mat. Par., V., p. 448; VI., p. 302. Rymer, I., p. 302.

[5] Rymer, I., p. 302. Burt., p. 340.

[6] Rymer, I., p. 297.

[7] *Ibid.*, p. 301. May 14, 1254.

issued the first[1] of a long line of extortionate bulls. The archbishop of Canterbury and the bishop of Chichester were ordered to borrow in the name of the pope and the churches of England as large a sum as possible from any who would lend, to bind the church in England to repayment, and to coerce all refractory churches and ecclesiastics of every degree by the severest spiritual penalties.

The league of Henry and Innocent was the league of inordinate vanity and visionary ambition with unbounded avarice and calculating selfishness. At the very moment when Albert sealed the concession of the 6th of March, negotiations were pending[2] between Innocent and Conrad; the pope throughout played his double game coolly and with consummate skill. Henry, however, was so elated by the pope's shadowy promise that by voice, smile, and gesture he proclaimed his exultation, and saluted Edmund openly as king. The first flush of enthusiasm boded ill to England, for Henry sent at once to Rome all the money he had in the treasury, all he could borrow from Richard of Cornwall, wring from the Jews, extort from the land by the itinerant-justices, and then promised to send more.[3]

The week following Innocent's formal ratification of the Sicilian compact, the Hohenstaufen cause received a heavy blow in Conrad's death. A fever, conceived in the autumn of the year before and heightened by

---

[1] Rymer, I., p. 301.
[2] Raynaldus, 1254, XII. Mansi, T. II., XXI., p. 512. Von Raumer, IV., pp. 194, 196.
[3] Mat. Par., V., p. 458.

grief, carried him off on the 21st of May,[1] 1254. Innocent's opponents in Italy were now limited to Conradin, Conrad's heir, a boy too young to inspire fear, and whose interests were managed by his friends; to Manfred, now simple prince of Tarentum; and to Berthold of Hohenburg, the leader of the German mercenaries. Through Manfred's shrewd concession, the latter held the whole administration in his grasp. When, in accordance with the dead Conrad's wishes, Berthold presented Conradin's cause to the pope, Innocent replied that the kingdom of Sicily belonged to himself, but that he would admit Conradin to favour in so far as his tender years would allow. Berthold was shrewd enough to see that if a papal army once entered Apulia, both his own power and Conradin's cause would be lost; he therefore leagued himself with Manfred. The latter governed in Conradin's name and was recognized by the magnates of Sicily as Conradin's lawful successor.[2] As soon as this was known, Innocent appointed a short respite, and at its expiration banned Manfred, Berthold, and all of their adherents who had failed to make submission.[3]

While still negotiating with Manfred and the rest, Innocent was straining every nerve to make the most of the advantage which had accrued to him by the decentralization of his opponent's power. On the 22d of May he ordered Henry to refrain from all unneces-

---

[1] Mat. Par., V., p. 460, n. 2. Böhmer, Regesta, p. 28. Von Raumer, IV., p. 196.
[2] Mat. Par., V., pp. 460, 461.
[3] Von Raumer, IV., pp. 199-201.

sary expenses, and caused Henry's counsellors to add their entreaties to his.[1] The next day he promised to pay £50,000 Tours immediately to Henry's agents at Lyons and to duplicate the sum later under certain conditions.[2] On the same day he extended the grant of the tenth for the crusade from three years to five,[3] and ordered the papal agents in Scotland to proceed to the more hasty collection of the twentieth which had there been granted[4] to Henry by the pope for the same purpose. All signs show that Innocent believed that his game was won already: joyfully he wrote that with the death of Conrad the last obstacle had vanished; that if Edmund would come with a suitable army, he would meet with no resistance; and he ordered Henry to prepare a great seal in readiness for the formal acceptance of the kingdom on September 29th.[5] He even refused Henry's request that his vow of a crusade to Palestine be commuted for the Sicilian expedition— "for," said the pope, "Sicily would be a fine stepping-stone in carrying out the former project."[6] A little later he wrote from Anagnia, urging Henry not to be remiss; that the Lord was with him and was making his way unexpectedly easy.[7] In this foretaste of

---

[1] Bulls to Henry, the queen, Peter of Savoy, in Rymer, I., pp. 302, 303.

[2] Rymer, I., p. 303. May 23, 1254.

[3] Rymer, I., p. 303. Original grant for three years, Rymer, I., p. 272. Ratification by English magnates in 1253, Mat. Par., V., pp. 374, 375. Ant. Leg., p. 18. Dunst., p. 190. Burt., p. 305.

[4] Rymer, I., p. 303.   [5] *Ibid.* Bulls of May, 1254.

[6] Rymer, I., p. 304.   [7] *Ibid.* June 9, 1254.

triumph Henry undoubtedly shared, for on the 3d of October he confirmed Edmund's grant[1] of Capua to Thomas of Savoy, and eleven days later he ordered the magnates of Sicily to pay homage to his envoys in the name of Edmund.[2]

On the 5th of September, Innocent had placed Cardinal Fiesco in charge of all Apulian matters.[3] By means of Henry's former gifts, and of loans from Italian merchants to whom the king was bound in payment, Innocent had raised an army of unwarlike and treacherous Italians and sent them forth, ostensibly to battle for the church.[4]

Manfred, in truth, had been hard pressed, though not by papal armies. His money was exhausted, and the German mercenaries had therefore become as dangerous as open enemies. Peter Rufus, too, the administrator of the island Sicily, had shown signs of yielding to the pope. Therefore, when Innocent's army was at hand, Manfred resolved to make a virtue of necessity, and himself led the pontiff to Naples. Peace was signed between them Sept. 27, 1254.[5] It mattered little to the pope that Edmund's seal for the acceptance of Sicily had been ordered for the 29th.[6] Obligations sat

---

[1] Rymer, I., p. 308.

[2] *Ibid.*, p. 310. Hereford and York.

[3] Von Raumer, IV., p. 201.

[4] Mat. Par., V., pp. 458, 459, 470. Ipse enim rex omnia ei abundanter necessaria ex inexhausto Angliæ puteo ministrabat. *Vide* also Rymer, I., p. 307. Bull of September 9th, concerning loan of Sienese merchants to the church of Cashel.

[5] Raynaldus, 1254, LVIII.-LX. Mansi, T. II., XXI., pp. 511, 512. Von Raumer, IV., p. 202. [6] Rymer, I., p. 303.

lightly on him, for his game seemed won. He was ruling at Naples, and all the Sicilian nobles were his very humble servants.[1] But this fair sky soon clouded. Manfred felt that Conradin and he were not treated as the sons of an emperor should be; his former opponents had more influence in every way than he himself; and the pope's dealings with England also came to light. The Burillo [2] episode precipitated matters. On the 17th of November, Innocent sent Henry the following significant message: "God has granted us a good beginning and things prosper. Our mandates are received submissively. But because the church by reason of the gentleness and sweetness of its rule cannot long govern here with efficacy, you must make haste to support it and not delay. With but a slight exertion the prize is yours; delay may ruin all." Then Innocent for the first time adds a threat: "I will you to know that the church can suffer no long postponement or delay, without herself providing for the matter and ceding the kingdom to another." [3] That very month, through fear of intrigue, Manfred entered Luceria and found there men, money, and material for war. Deserters from the papal army kept flocking to his stand-

[1] Rymer, I., p. 312. Mandata nostra suscipiuntur humiliter et servantur. Cf. Nangis, I., p. 210. Berthold had yielded in November and been made seneschal of Apulia; other grants were also given to himself and brothers. Rymer, I., pp. 311, 312. Confirmation by Alexander IV., Rymer, I., p. 314. February, 1255.

[2] Von Raumer, IV., pp. 203-205.

[3] Rymer, I., p. 312. Sciturus pro certo, quod ecclesia multum differre vel expectare non posset, quin super re illa, et de concedendo ipsam alteri aliter provideret.

ard, and he grew stronger day by day. Instead of at once advancing against him and cutting off supplies, Fiesco preached crusades. The favourable moment passed, and on the 2d of December Manfred's victory at Foggia over Otto, Berthold's brother, gave the papal cause decisive check. As soon as the news arrived, Fiesco's army bolted in wildest confusion, Apulia was left unprotected, and when the new year dawned, the whole province, with the exception of Otranto, was in Manfred's hands.[1] Such was the campaign on which Henry had lavished English treasure.

On the 13th of December, from chagrin or chronic disease, Innocent IV. had died — four years to a day from the ill-starred Frederic's death.[2] It was said that during his pontificate he had impoverished the church universal more than had all his predecessors together from the earliest times[3] — a melancholy epitaph for the failure of a life.

From his temperate, kindly, and religious successor, England expected much. But in those days a pope could no more refrain from extortion than he could be a Ghibelline. On his death-bed Innocent had urged the cardinals to continue the war against Manfred, and papal policy made it appear that care for Henry's interests was a prominent factor in their subsequent deliberations.[4] On this basis Alexander IV. became a very Rehoboam.

---

[1] Von Raumer, IV., pp. 211–214, 216.
[2] Rymer, I., p. 312. Cf. von Raumer, IV., p. 215, n. 3.
[3] Mat. Par., V., p. 355, quoting Grosseteste.
[4] Cf. Mat. Par., V., pp. 472, 473.

The new pope had found diplomacy a very tangled web. At the end of February, or a little later, he was forced to seek negotiations with Manfred; he had already given a written promise to Conradin's grandmother, mother, and uncles, that he should have his rights and more.[1] Yet in defiance of common honesty, he had at the same time been dealing with Henry's plenipotentiary, the bishop of Hereford, and on the 9th of April a treaty[2] was formally concluded. It is needless to say that the terms were sufficiently in favour of the pope.

First, the kingdom of the Two Sicilies was never to be divided, and Edmund and his successors were to do liege homage to the See of Rome. Second, 2000 ounces of pure gold were to be paid yearly in token of subjection, and at the pope's requisition three hundred knights, equipped and maintained at the king's expense, were to be furnished for three months' service annually, anywhere in Italy. Third, churches, church-estates, and all ecclesiastics were to enjoy canonical rights, and the authority of the pope in respect to them was in all cases to be allowed free exercise. To the king was saved such customary rights of patronage as were not uncanonical. Fourth, full restitution was to be made by the king to all the clergy who had been dispossessed. Fifth, on penalty of forfeiture and excommunication no election to the headship of the empire was to be sought or accepted. Sixth, Beneventum was

---

[1] Von Raumer, IV., pp. 216, 217, 219. Jan. 23, 1255.
[2] Rymer, I., pp. 316-318. Naples, April 9, 1255.

to be reserved to the pope; all claim on the £100,-000 Tours promised by Innocent[1] was to be relinquished; and all honours and donations[2] to the Hohenburgs and others were to be confirmed. Seventh, Henry should bind himself and his whole kingdom to repay the 135,541 marks already spent by the pope in the acquisition of Sicily, and also to repay all expenses still to be incurred. The first amount was to be discharged before Sept. 29, 1256. Eighth, after the full payment of the foregoing, and not earlier, Henry was to send a captain and an army to Apulia — but in no case later than Sept. 29, 1256. Ninth, in case of failure to fulfil these terms, the penalty was forfeiture of the kingdom, excommunication, and an interdict on England. Tenth, the pope reserved to himself the right to make such further grants as seemed essential. Any surplus of income from Sicily over the outgoes was to be restored to Edmund, but no account should be required.

This final clause seems scarcely necessary, for Manfred was then in full possession of Calabria and Alexander was about to bind himself to pay the Hohenburgs 8000 ounces of gold in compensation for their losses.[3]

The immediate and most important effect of this treaty was the invasion of England by swarms of papal

---

[1] Rymer, I., p. 303. *Vide supra*, p. 121.
[2] They amounted to 7500 ounces of gold yearly.
[3] Rymer, I., p. 319. Bulls of May 19 and 21, 1255. Von Raumer, IV., p. 218.

emissaries. The bishop of Bologna arrived in early autumn, and on the 18th of October-formally invested Edmund with the kingdom by a ring, and received his homage. On the same day Henry ordered John Mansel to seal the writ of acceptance.[1] The pope was now legally clothed with all the rights and powers of an acknowledged creditor — and that to an unlimited extent.

The bishop of Hereford had also returned. During his stay in Rome he had introduced an exceedingly ingenious method of extortion by means of what seems to have been the use of unauthorized bills of exchange. The chronicles of the time are full of his infamy in binding the church of England to Sienese and Florentine merchants by means of forged procurations. All burdens of days gone by seemed light in comparison with the present exaction.[2] With Hereford, Sept. 29, 1255, came the Gascon Rustand, a learned man,[3] most dangerous of legates. The number of the bulls he brought was legion. Luceria, the Saracen city founded by Frederic II., had long been a thorn in the pope's side; it had been a place of refuge for Conrad in his day and now served Manfred's turn. Under the pretext of destroying this relic of paganism, doubly

---

[1] Mat. Par., V., p. 515. Rymer, I., pp. 323, 324, 331, 332. The barons had neither part nor lot in this whole affair. *Vide* Rymer, I., p. 373.

[2] Mat. Par., V., pp. 510, 512. Dunst., p. 199. Burt., pp. 348, 349, 361. Osney, p. 109. Wykes, p. 126.

[3] Mat. Par., V., p. 519. Burt., p. 350. Dunst., p. 196. Oxenedes, p. 205. Homo litteratus et efficax ad nocendum.

dangerous because so near the holy city of the popes, Rustand was ordered to preach a general crusade against Manfred, and to promise to all participants the privileges and immunities granted in the general Council of Lyons to crusaders;[1] to commute Henry's vow of a regular crusade to a vow in favour of the Sicilian enterprise;[2] to collect and assign[3] to Henry's use all money raised, or to be raised, on the tenth for the crusade; and to assume full charge in England, Scotland, and Ireland of all matters which were in any way connected with the cross.[4] His assistant in the latter function was Bernard of Siena.[5]

Even before the bishop of Bologna had fulfilled his mission, matters in Italy had grown steadily worse for Henry and the pope. Cardinal Octavian, the leader of the Roman army, had been at first successful in his military operations — so wrote[6] the pope to Henry in the middle of September — but lately, on account of treachery[7] and guile, so many obstacles had been raised up against him, that he had been forced to retreat with all his army into Terra di Lavoro. There was need of urgent haste. The pope could no longer sustain so great a weight alone; he had exhausted his treasury, contracted innumerable debts, and so overstrained his

---

[1] Mat. Par., V., p. 474. Burt., p. 350. Rymer, I., p. 320.
[2] Rymer, I., p. 319. May 3, 1255.
[3] Burt., pp. 350, 351.
[4] *Ibid.*, pp. 350, 353.
[5] Rymer, I., p. 330. Oct. 12, 1255.
[6] Rymer, I., p. 328. Anagnia, Sept. 18, 1255.
[7] Cf. Mat. Par., V., pp. 474, 498.

credit that no further loans could be obtained. He therefore exhorted Henry to send an army immediately, while Sicily and that part of the mainland which offered easiest access to the rest was still in his power. If Terra di Lavoro were once lost, the greatest efforts could scarcely win it back. Such was the bad news which Henry was destined to receive from the hands of John de Dya, papal emissary.[1] Neither a letter nor English gold availed to stem the tide: by the following February Terra di Lavoro had fallen, and Manfred was practically lord of the land. In 1257 the pope's power was scarcely mentioned there, and in the ensuing year Manfred was solemnly crowned king.[2]

Throughout the autumn Henry was still ignorant of his great misfortune, and Rustand's mission went merrily on. His crusade-preaching, however, was neither successful nor popular. In truth, in England the crusading-idea had long since worn itself out. Gains obtained from oppression and the impoverishment of the poor were displeasing in the sight of God, and their subsequent expenditure was not blessed with his favour, so people thought.[3]

For the same reasons, Rustand's exactions were doubly unwelcome. He demanded redemption-money from crusaders, and extended the tenth for the crusade through two years more.[4] The tenth was to be assessed

---

[1] Rymer, I., p. 328.   [2] Von Raumer, IV., p. 225.

[3] Cf. Mat. Par., V., pp. 170, 171, 522. End of one of Rustand's sermons: "Estote filii obedientiæ. Obligamini tali et tali mercatori, in tanta pecuniæ quantitate." This is seldom a popular style.

[4] Bulls in Burt., pp. 350, 351. Rymer, I., p. 303.

according to a new and stringent valuation,¹ and was to embrace the income from manors and baronies — on the ground that "one-tenth of ecclesiastical income" included the income from baronies and manors under the control of churches or ecclesiastics.² If all demands were not paid in full by the 2d of February, 1256, delinquents were declared to be guilty of fraud and *ipso facto* excommunicated. The shortness of the time was in itself a heavy grievance, for churches were thereby compelled to borrow at ruinous rates of interest from the usurers whom Rustand's foresight had provided.³

His exactions came at the worst possible time for king and realm. Henry's Gascon expedition had entailed a debt of 350,000 marks.⁴ His consequent extortions had driven all classes wild.⁵ The demand for the three great officers of state, made for the first time in 1244 and renewed in 1248 and 1249, had been repeated and refused in the Hokeday parliament⁶ of 1255, and when the magnates reassembled, on the 13th of October, their temper was obdurate. The king demanded an aid — first from Richard of Cornwall, who refused chiefly because the king had assumed the Sicilian business without his advice and the consent of the baronage,

---

¹ Burt., pp. 356–360. Item, nulla sit portio adeo modica, in quibuscumque consistat in pondere, numero, et mensura, terris, pratis, pascuis, pannagiis, auro, argento, grano, liquore, operibus, servitiis liberis vel rusticis consuetudinibus, in panibus deferendis ad Natale Domini, gallinis, ovis, et quibuscumque aliis ad ecclesias vel ecclesiasticas personas spectantibus, quin taxetur et æstimetur, etc.

² Burt., p. 354. ³ Mat. Par., V., p. 530.
⁴ *Ibid.*, p. 521. ⁵ Cf. Mat. Par., V., pp. 104, 105.
⁶ April 6th. Mat. Par., V., p. 494. Burt., p. 336.

and next from the other magnates. They also refused, assigning the portentous reason that all had not been summoned according to the terms of the Great Charter.¹ It was evident that a period of constitutional resistance was at hand.

Rustand, meanwhile, had summoned a convocation of the clergy to assemble also on the 13th of October, and had laid his demands before them. He, too, met with resistance: Fulk of London, and Walter of Worcester, a prelate endowed with Grosseteste's spirit, and like him a warm friend of Simon de Montfort,² headed the opposition. Their task was difficult in the extreme. The archbishop of Canterbury was absent, York was dead, and Winchester distrusted, while Rustand and Henry were in formal alliance. The clergy, therefore, postponed their answer till Jan. 13, 1256, appealed by letter to the pope, and separated in distress, without having agreed upon any definite line of action.³

Their appeal was based upon the following grievances.⁴ First, a tenth of their income had been granted arbitrarily to the king, although their own expressed consent was necessary.⁵ Second, the tenth had been conceded for a definite use, time, and cause, all three of which had now been changed. The clergy were

---

[1] Mat. Par., V., pp. 520, 521. Burt., p. 360.

[2] Mon. Fran., Ep. Ad., CXLI., p. 270. Adam to Leicester. Concepi autem spem indubitatem in Domino quod illud bene prosperabitur per sollicitudinem dom. Lincolniæ et dom. Wygorniæ, vobis inter mortales omnes speciali amicitia favorabiliores.

[3] Mat. Par., V., pp. 524, 525 *et seq.* Burt., p. 360.

[4] Burt., pp. 360-363.   [5] Cf. Burt., p. 356.

therefore not bound to pay, especially since the present use was not even dreamed of at the time of the grant.[1] Third, their manors and baronies were twice taxed, — once by the king for military service, and again by the pope for the disme. Fourth, in defiance of precedent and custom the clergy were compelled to pay strange taxes of all kinds, and that by a yearly assessment under oath. Fifth, Rustand, by giving his proxies to underlings,[2] by summoning individuals to crusade-courts held in remote places, and by encroachments on the jurisdiction of the ordinaries, misused his powers. Sixth, doubtful legacies, heretofore employed for relief of the poor, maintenance of hospitals, and other purposes, were now granted to the king, although lay abuses of the church exceeded even those practised before the Charters of Liberty had been confirmed. Seventh, the extent of the taxation was too great; even where benefices scarcely supported their incumbents, the tithe was still taken. Eighth, Hereford's forged procurations were roundly denounced, and a vigorous protest against the whole Sicilian affair was made, — on the ground that it was undertaken by traitorous advice. A general declaration that the clergy were willing to support the See of Rome in all lawful enterprises may have slightly weakened the force of the appeal.

During the interim which lay between the October

---

[1] April, 1253. Mat. Par., V., pp. 374, 375.

[2] Cf. Mat. Par., V., p. 536. Datur potestas personis prorsus indignis super nobiles ecclesias et eorum prælatos excellentes.

and January convocations, news had arrived of Octavian's defeat[1] and of Manfred's brilliant successes, yet the king persisted in his folly, and lavished gifts upon the foreigners in England.[2] At length the prelates met to give Rustand his final answer. A certain master Leonard was their spokesman. When Rustand arrogantly said that all churches belonged to the pope, Leonard, possibly remembering the words of Grosseteste,[3] made answer: "True — but for protection, not revenue or appropriation. Such was the intention of the founders." In anger Rustand then ordered each man to speak for himself, that the pope and king might know their individual opinions. He had already drafted a document which asserted that the prelates had received a "loan for the advantage of their churches;" since he would not alter it, the prelates again appealed, and sent a formal embassy to Rome.[4] The Magna Charta and John's Charter to the church were rehearsed, and their observance ordered; but although the king was ruthlessly sacking vacant churches, the pope returned the answer that in these days he would not offend princes.[5]

No definite answer had yet been given by the prelates. Rustand had weakened somewhat under the threat of appeal, and on the 29th of January had miti-

---

[1] *Vide supra*, pp. 123–124, 128–129.
[2] Mat. Par., V., pp. 521, 531, 536.
[3] Cf. Mat. Par., V., p. 536. Also Rob. Gross., Epist. CXXVIII., p. 437. Hæc enim est potestatis plenitudo, omnia posse in ædificationem.
[4] Mat. Par., V., pp. 539, 540. [5] *Ibid.*, pp. 540–544.

gated the taxation by exempting houses for the poor and hospitals, and he forbade his proctors to trespass on the jurisdiction of the ordinaries. To all who paid the tenth he also granted the same privileges which were accorded to crusaders,[1] — a sure sign that the money was coming in but slowly. At the same time came the reply from the pope to the bishops' first appeal. They were ordered to pay the merchants to whom the church was bound, but were allowed to withhold a corresponding amount from the tithes, — an empty privilege. In this way the church was tallaged.[2]

Two weeks after Easter, 1256, the bishops for the third time assembled at London to give Rustand his final answer. At first, in their great dejection, they were on the point of yielding, but encouragement came from the barons, and the clergy boldly replied that Henry should have nothing from their baronies.[3] This was a turning-point in the history of the reign. The barons, six months before, had adopted the line of strict constitutional resistance; on similar grounds, driven by royal and papal aggressions, the patriotic wing of the clergy was now compelled to join them. To a prophetic eye the parliament of Oxford was looming in the distance.

The king was now forced to exactions of a meaner kind. All men who possessed twenty-five librates of

---

[1] Mat. Par., V., p. 540. Burt., pp. 363, 364.
[2] Mat. Par., V., p. 558. Burt., p. 364.
[3] Mat. Par., V., p. 553.

land were compelled to take up their knighthood or pay a money-fine.[1] From the Cistercians of Reading he demanded, through Rustand, a sum equal to the whole value of their stock of wool, their sole means of maintenance. They courageously refused to pay, and for once the pope stood firm to a previous indulgence and confirmed their privilege. From individual abbots of the order, however, Rustand succeeded in extorting some money before the papal bull arrived.[2] Meanwhile Manfred was winning his kingdom, and the English people were learning to detest the very names of king and pope.

Before the decisive Easter meeting of the prelates had occurred, Alexander had written[3] to Hereford that Henry's negligence was causing his Italian creditors to harass and annoy the pope, and that they would certainly seize their surety, if not paid within the stipulated time. A whole province was now threatened by the enemy; instant aid would save it at but slight expense; if once lost, the greatest outlay of strength and money could scarcely win it back. An emphatic postscript stated that unless all debts were paid within the time appointed, the pope would forthwith nullify the compact and give the kingdom to another.

If Alexander's lines had fallen in unpleasant places, Henry fared still worse. He had to bear debt, losses,

---

[1] Mat. Par., V., p. 560.
[2] *Ibid.*, pp. 553–555, 557. Rymer, I., p. 323. Waverley, p. 348.
[3] Rymer, I., p. 336, Feb. 5, 1256. The province was Terra di Lavoro, and the time was Sept. 29, 1256.

and reproaches from the pope, to tread the way of the transgressor, which is proverbially hard, and to fear in addition the opposition of his magnates. On the 15th of February the warden of Dover was ordered to allow no clerk to cross the Channel unless he first swore that, if he went to Rome, he would attempt nothing to the injury of the king or to the detriment of the Sicilian enterprise.[1] As soon as Henry learned of the refusal of the prelates and magnates to come to his assistance, he wrote[2] to William Bonquer, his agent at Rome, stating that on account of Octavian's failure and the capture of the count of Savoy at Turin, he could not pay his debt nor send an army within the stipulated time. At the same time he wrote[3] to Alexander and the cardinals, that in view of the requirement of military aid and of the great sums which he already owed to Rome, his council refused to sanction the Sicilian enterprise, and the prelates refused to pay Rustand. All were afraid to undertake the business in this state, for failure seemed certain, and the stipulated time was short. He therefore sought a prolongation. This was afterwards granted, reluctantly, and with bitter reproaches.[4]

After the loss of Terra di Lavoro, the pope redoubled

---

[1] Rymer, I., p. 337.

[2] *Ibid.* Shirley, II., pp. 114-116.

[3] Rymer, I., pp. 337-339, March 27, 1256. Non enim credimus quod hodie princeps aliquis regnat in terris, qui ita subito tantam pecuniam possit habere ad manum.

[4] Rymer, I., p. 342. Other prolongations, Rymer, I., pp. 350, 366, 369.

his almost hopeless efforts. Rustand was informed that the clergy must pay the tenth, even if double taxation were thereby entailed.[1] At Henry's request, Alexander also granted him through Rustand the revenue of all vacant benefices whose collation pertained to the pope, the incomes of all non-resident incumbents,[2] and the goods of intestates which fell to the church.[3] In spite of the prelates' petition, the true valuation obtained on oath — "taxatione antiqua nequaquam obstante"— was reaffirmed as the basis of taxation.

To crown the evils of this most wretched year, the Welsh rebelled about the time of harvest, and defied the utmost efforts of Prince Edward to reduce them to a state of peace.[4]

The year 1257 was ushered in by a second attempt at extortion from the unfortunate Cistercians, and again they plead their privileges. Henry promptly commanded that no favour should be shown to the order, — a virtual sentence of outlawry, — and the sheriffs and judges of the forest-courts were permitted to despoil them.[5]

About Lent, another envoy, John of Messina, arrived from Rome.[6] With him he brought a bull of prolongation, accusation, and incitement to action.[7] As if the

---

[1] Rymer, I., p. 342. June 13, 1256.
[2] Rymer, I., pp. 344, 345. Aug. 21, 1256.
[3] Rymer, I., p. 345.
[4] Mat. Par., V., p. 592. *Vide infra*, Part VIII.
[5] Mat. Par., V., p. 610. January 6th.
[6] Mat. Par., V., p. 614.
[7] Rymer, I., p. 351. Messina's commission. Nov. 9, 1256.

pope had been granting Henry the greatest favour in the world, he wrote that he had assumed full charge of the Sicilian enterprise, raised armies, and sent legates to command them, yet Henry was relax. If the king failed, it would be not only disgraceful to Henry himself, but disastrous to his reputation throughout Europe for military power. The king was therefore ordered to reconcile to himself all those prelates whose rights had been infringed, as well as all other persons whose aid might be of value. It could scarcely have been in furtherance of this latter task that Messina bore also papal letters of authorization for collecting and receiving money, and for punishing delinquents. At once he issued imperious summons to the prelates. His mode of dealing with them may be gathered from his treatment of St. Albans. He had demanded procurations from the abbey, and since the monks who came in response to his summons failed to bring them, he detained the monks by force until they had signed bills on merchants to the amount of twenty-one marks.[1] Rustand's powers had at this same time been greatly amplified, — a rare measure of conciliation, — and that no stimulus to Henry's activity might be wanting, the Roman court had sown broadcast the accusation that Manfred sought to murder both Henry and his sons.[2]

All the new schemes for extortion were brought to light at a mid-Lent parliament in London. Nearly all the nobility of England were present, and the city could

---

[1] Mat. Par., V., pp. 614, 615.
[2] Cf. Burt., p. 395.

scarcely contain the vast throngs.¹ On the 2d of April, at Westminster, Rustand proclaimed to the archdeacons of all England the authority ² with which he was now clothed: first, absolute power, without appeal, over all cases involving crusaders and legacies, clear or doubtful, for the Holy Land; second, power of inquiry concerning all benefices so long vacant that their collation devolved on the pope; third, visitatorial power over clerks who held a plurality of benefices, the final decision of such cases being reserved to the pope; fourth, power to collect all the income of non-resident incumbents; fifth, to collect for five years the first-fruits of all vacant benefices — bishoprics and regular prelacies excepted; sixth, power to compel the archdeacons to collect the tenth for the two additional years at the new valuation. Lastly, power was given to the bishop of Norwich, the elect of Salisbury, and Rustand himself to make all arrangements concerning the disme. After some deliberation it was decided that a definite answer should be given within a month after Easter or Rustand should proceed.³

On the same day the archbishop of Messina had made an address to the magnates — prelates, clergy, and laymen — on the Sicilian affair, endeavouring to persuade them to assume the enterprise and help the king.⁴ After a few days' deliberation — in the course of which the archbishop demanded procurations from

---

[1] Mat. Par., V., pp. 621, 622.
[2] Burt., pp. 388, 389.
[3] *Ibid.*, p. 389. [4] *Ibid.*, p. 386.

the archdeacons[1] — the king and Messina received an answer.[2] It was written in French and Latin; its title read, "Reasons of the Magnates against the King." Sicily's remoteness, the danger in traversing hostile countries to reach it, Manfred's occupation of Calabria and the keys of the kingdom, his popularity and wealth, were first mentioned. The enormous outlays which Henry had already made in vain, and the vast expenses which would be necessary in the future, were next instanced. The realm was in no condition to meet them, for king and people were alike impoverished, royal officials were plundering the land, disturbances were brewing in Gascony, Ireland, and Scotland, while the Welsh were in open rebellion. That in case the expedition were undertaken England would lie naked to its enemies, especially to France, and that on account of the hard conditions imposed by the pontiff, the king might at any moment forfeit the crown, were the final and conclusive arguments.

At the formal session of parliament the king introduced Edmund, dressed in Apulian costume, and implored the magnates for aid. He stated the amount of the sum for which he was bound, asked that the tenth be granted for the full five years at the new valuation, requested the concession for five years of the first-fruits of vacant benefices, also one-half the income of nonresident incumbents, all the revenue of privileged pluralists, except from one benefice which they should

---

[1] Burt., pp. 389, 390.
[2] *Ibid.*, pp. 386, 387. Cf. Dunst., p. 200.

reserve, and finally all doubtful legacies.¹ The clergy gave excellent reasons² for refusing this extortion, but on the king's promise to confirm and keep the Charters, they finally granted him 52,000 marks. It was the richest gift the king had ever had, but he received it churlishly.³ That he might know the burdens of the church and ensure the relief which he had promised, the prelates drew up their fifty articles of grievances.⁴

The archbishop of Messina left for Rome in May, having completed all arrangements for the sending of an army.⁵ Meanwhile papal exactions continued. Henry's faith in his ultimate success, however, seemed now for the first time to waver.⁶ He ordered Rustand to pay no more debts on the Sicilian account until he himself had better security; the pope was forced to allege his recent banning of Manfred as a proof of his good intentions.⁷ Again, in a number of documents, Henry at this time sought a mitigation of the pope's conditions, and even authorized ambassadors to renounce the business altogether, if it seemed to them expedient.⁸ Above all, he relinquished his darling plan of conquering France by way of Poitou, Sicily, and

---

¹ Mat. Par., V., p. 623. Burt., p. 390. Osney, p. 114. Wykes, pp. 126, 127.
² Burt., pp. 390, 391.
³ Mat. Par., V., pp. 624, 637.
⁴ *Ibid.*, p. 638; VI., pp. 353-365.
⁵ Rymer, I., p. 355. Cf. Burt., p. 400.
⁶ Cf. Mat. Par., V., p. 643.
⁷ Rymer, I., pp. 356, 357. June 3, 1257.
⁸ *Ibid.*, pp. 359, 360. June 26th and 28th.

Germany, and sent envoys, at the pope's request, to negotiate a final peace.[1]

About this time another gleam of light for England appeared on the horizon. Rustand had made the most of his private opportunities, and become not the least wealthy man in the kingdom. The prelates complained to the pope, aroused his jealous indignation, and procured the recall of the hated envoy.[2]

It is evident that Henry had not lost heart completely, however, for on the 28th of June he sent a letter[3] of excuses to the pope: he had not paid his debts in full, because of the constant troubles which he had had, and was still having, with the recalcitrant prelates; he could not send an army, because he had not paid the debts, and because the Welsh rebellion, in connection with his Gascon reverses, had paralyzed his strength. He asked for further time. Meanwhile his expenses still kept on and interest was rapidly accumulating. On the 5th of May his envoys at Rome had contracted a loan at no less a rate than five per cent per month.[4] Fugitives from Apulia also began to come in, recommended by the pope to Henry's fostering care on the ground that they had suffered in the latter's service.[5] Even at the beginning of 1258, Henry realized his position so little, that he wrote to Cardinal Octavian

---

[1] Rymer, I., pp. 355, 358, 359.

[2] Mat. Par., V., p. 647. Dunst., p. 206.

[3] Rymer, I., pp. 359, 360.

[4] *Ibid.*, p. 365. Per singulos duos menses, pro singulis decem marcis, unam marcam.

[5] *Ibid.*, p. 366.

that notwithstanding the refusal of the barons to sanction the Sicilian enterprise, he yet hoped to find means to bring it to a successful conclusion.[1]

The pope was still more completely in the dark. About the middle of Lent Rustand returned, with diminished powers it is true, but with him was an envoy named Herlot, bringing confusion to the church of England.[2] The full effect of Herlot's mission was not felt even in England until the parliament of Hokeday met, and it was much longer before the pope could know it. As late as the 28th of December, 1258, Alexander wrote[3] to Henry in threatening language that, unless the terms were fulfilled, the concession of Sicily would be forthwith rescinded. Matters were then in stronger hands than his. The exactions of the pope and king had been rousing for long years the patriots of England — church, baronage, and people — to resistance; the royal system of administration, which had dispensed with the three great officers of state and governed by commissions of pliable underlings, had caused the resistance to take a constitutional form with Magna Charta as its basis; the royal policy which throughout the reign had favoured non-national objects abroad and at home, and which had found its most congenial expression in wars for conquest and in the introduction of aliens, had made the spirit of resistance no less

---

[1] Shirley, II., p. 126. January or February, 1258.
[2] Mat. Par., V., p. 672. Dunst., p. 208. Burt., p. 409. Theok., p. 163.
[3] Rymer, I., pp. 379, 380.

national than constitutional; the royal tyranny and caprice had alienated from the crown the one man, above all others, who was most competent to guide the national movement and the most likely to place it on a popular basis; the Sicilian enterprise had revealed the depth of the king's incapacity and of his treason to his people, outraged public feeling beyond measure, and was in itself an ample reason for armed resistance. Therefore, as soon as the Welsh war had proved the king's military weakness and furnished the barons a pretext for appearing in arms,[1] the movement acquired irresistible force. Before Alexander had dictated his last demand for money in the year 1258, Manfred was reigning supreme in the kingdom of the Two Sicilies, and a committee of the barons and prelates of England was holding daily sessions in the New Temple at London, ruling the land as the lawful representatives of the three estates of the realm.

---

[1] Mat. Par., V., p. 696. Rish., Chronicon, p. 8. Burt., p. 438.

PART VIII

THE WELSH WAR, AND THE FAMINE OF THE YEAR 1258

THROUGHOUT the whole reign of Henry III. there had been more or less trouble with the Welsh, and the king's success in dealing with them had been slight. It is difficult to assess upon each party its due amount of blame for aggressions: the very existence of a March system, on the one hand, which at the time of its establishment had assured to an encroaching baron the lands which he conquered, was a constant menace to a state of peace, while on the other hand the Welsh were but partly civilized, and their poverty must have constantly tempted them to raids for which their rocky fastnesses promised them impunity. In the great rebellion of the year 1256, however, the case is much clearer than usual. While in England the spirit of nationality had been steadily growing in intensity, a parallel movement had been occurring in Wales. The discord which existed between Henry and his barons and among the barons themselves, had given the Welsh a deep impression of England's military weakness. It was a direct encroachment on their national rights which fanned the spark of national enthusiasm into a consuming fire.

Shortly after Edward's marriage to the princess of

Castile, Henry had given him a magnificent appanage,[1] in which was included the overlordship of the conquered parts of Wales. At the end of November, 1255, Edward had returned to England,[2] and through his agent, Geoffrey of Langley, had begun at once to collect his revenues. Geoffrey had acquired already, in the service of the king, an exceedingly unenviable reputation for extortion,[3] but in Wales he fairly surpassed himself. Not content with the ordinary sources of revenue, he levied an unprecedented capitation-tax, and in addition sought to introduce English laws and territorial divisions.[4] About the 1st of November,[5] 1256, the Welsh broke out in rebellion, and assigned to it the broad basis of national rights and existence. They refused to acknowledge Edward as their lord, demanded the preservation of their ancient customs, and swore rather to die for the liberty of their country than to live in dishonourable subjection.[6] They passed their boundaries

---

[1] Dunst., p. 194. Rymer, I., pp. 296, 297. Feb. 14, 1254.

[2] Ant. Leg., p. 23. November 29th.

[3] Mat. Par., V., pp. 136, 137, 340.

[4] Dunst., p. 200. Theok., p. 158.

[5] Mat. Par., V., p. 592. Cf. Pauli, Gesch. von Eng., III., p. 705. Pauli, on the strength of a letter written by Peter de Montfort, the custodian of certain castles on the Welsh border (Mem. 2. Ann. Hen. III., p. 41, September 25th), dates the beginning of the revolt at the end of September, 1256. This letter, however, is addressed to "Monsire Phelippe Basset, justice de Engleterre," and must therefore be referred to the year 1262. Cf. Rymer, I., p. 339. Shirley, II., pp. 219-221. Ant. Leg., p. 49. Wykes, p. 129. Mat. West., pp. 380, 381. Dunst., p. 217. Rish., Chronica, p. 10. The same letter misleads Pauli also as to the extent of the incursion.

[6] Mat. Par., V., pp. 592, 596. Ant. Leg., p. 29. Theok., p. 158. Dunst., p. 201.

at once, attacked Edward's lands and castles, and marched as far as Chester, pillaging and laying waste. So great was their success that they were believed to have received secret aid from certain of the Marchers who were not sorry in this way to check the king's attempts on English liberty.¹ Edward fled before the Welsh to Richard at Wallingford, and borrowed from him 4000 marks with which to carry on the war; but the winter was wet and boisterous, the English forces failed to penetrate the pathless marshes and fastnesses of Wales,² and he lost his money and his pains. The manly conduct of the Welsh did not fail to elicit the admiration even of their foes,³ — at that time doubtless in a frame of mind which could appreciate the nobility of a struggle for national rights against the encroachments of aliens.

Every attempt on the part of Henry, Edward, and Richard to secure a truce, failed; the Welsh were in league with the weather and helped by England's foreign complications. Henry could give Edward no assistance, because his energies were paralyzed by his Sicilian troubles. He therefore roughly bade the prince "exert his untried strength, kindle his youthful ardour, and make his enemies afraid of him forevermore."⁴ Henry's version of "Let the boy win his spurs" was singularly unheroic. Richard of Cornwall refused to

---

¹ *Vide* Mat. Par., V., pp. 592, 594, 597, 598. Wykes, p. 111. The report was probably false, as the next year showed.

² Mat. Par., V., pp. 593, 594.

³ *Ibid.*, pp. 596, 597, 639.   ⁴ *Ibid.*, pp. 597, 614.

send good money after bad; as the sole result of her war with Turin the queen's exchequer was empty; and the Welsh therefore continued through the winter to plunder, burn, and kill, without let or hindrance.¹

Early in May, 1257, Edward summoned forces from Ireland, but the Welsh prepared to resist them at sea. The barons of the March attempted an expedition, but it was caught between a wood and a marsh, and few returned to tell the tale.² The peril, in truth, was great; for the first time in the memory of man North and South Wales were united in resistance and attack. Henry was forced to summon³ the general levy of the realm and to take the field in person. One division of the English army was to march upon Chester and North Wales; the other, from Bristol towards the south. The 1st of August was the time appointed, and the king accompanied the former body. As the army approached Chester about harvest-time, it destroyed the standing crops lest they should fall into the enemies' hands. This, together with a refusal to treat for peace on the basis of the restoration to the Welsh of their ancient customs, was practically all that the campaign accomplished.⁴ As Henry advanced, the Welsh retreated with their wives and children to the inaccessible wilds of Snowdon, breaking down the bridges and

---

[1] Mat. Par., V., pp. 597, 633.
[2] *Ibid.*, VI., pp. 372, 373. Theok., p. 158. Burt., p. 408. Osney, p. 116. Wykes, p. 117.
[3] Rymer, I., p. 361. July 18, 1257.
[4] Mat. Par., V., pp. 647, 648. Theok., p. 158. Osney, p. 117. Wykes, p. 117.

deepening the fords.¹ The king penetrated as far as Gannoc Castle, spent there a month of inglorious inaction, and then began a still more inglorious retreat. The Welsh hung about the rear of the army, mocking the troops and cutting off stragglers, while the king, clad in magnificent armour, rode in the midst of his troops, beneath the great banner of England, and shouted with eager voice, "Kill me these Welshmen, these off-scourings of men."² Such, at least, is the pen-picture of a hostile chronicler.³ Henry was unable to defeat his enemies, but he had already established a precedent for consoling himself for his own losses. As previously he had practised extortion after his disastrous Gascon war, so he now burdened the land by collecting a heavy scutage.⁴

Although later in the year James of Aldithley led a more or less successful foray into Wales, it failed to re-establish the English power there, and the condition of the Marches grew steadily worse. The loss of the usual Welsh supplies of horses and cattle was already felt severely in England, and by the end of the year the borders of Wales were a desert.⁵ The Welsh still continued their forays, and when, in March, 1258, they formed a league⁶ with the discontented elements in

---

[1] Mat. Par., V., p. 639.
[2] *Ibid.*, pp. 649, 651. Dunst., p. 204. Theok., p. 158. Osney, p. 117. Wykes, p. 117. Burt., p. 408.
[3] Mat. Par. It is probably essentially correct.
[4] Theok., p. 158.
[5] Mat. Par., V., pp. 656, 657, 660.
[6] Rymer, I., p. 370. March 18th.

Scotland, the danger became more pressing than ever, and the dissatisfaction of the English with their king grew more pronounced.

That nothing might be wanting to excite them still further against the government, the very elements turned traitor to the king. Heavy rains in the autumn of 1257 had proved disastrous to the crops, and throughout the spring of the following year the north wind had blown continuously and blasted all the buds.[1] The scanty harvest of 1257 was soon exhausted, and a frightful famine broke out. The poor were reduced to eating horse-flesh, the bark of trees, or worse.[2] By the middle of May thousands had perished in London alone, although that city had been especially favoured.[3] In March, Richard had sent to England fifty vessels laden with German corn,[4] and this had been sold in open market. It had by no means redounded to Henry's popularity that he had endeavoured to seize it for his own use, and that the matter had been carried to the courts.[5] For the scarcity of crops, the king could not be censured justly; but then, as now, there existed a strong tendency in human nature to lay the blame for all agricultural mishaps at the government's door.

---

[1] Mat. Par., V., pp. 660, 661, 690.

[2] Taxster, *apud* Rish., Chronicon, Ed. Halliwell, p. 113; *apud* B. Cotton, p. 137.

[3] Mat. Par., V., pp. 693, 694. Quindecim milia. Fabyan, p. 343. Cf. Theok., p. 166.

[4] Mat. Par., V., pp. 673, 674.

[5] Ant. Leg., p. 37. Fabyan, p. 341. *Vide*, also, Pauli, Gesch. von Eng., III., p. 714 and n. 4.

And, undoubtedly, Henry was to blame for those exactions of his own and of the pope which had so drained the land of ready money that prices rose to an enormously exaggerated height. The poor were compelled thereby to eat the bread of charity or starve.[1] The crop of vengeance was the only harvest fully ripe.

---

[1] Mat. Par., V., pp. 673, 674, 728, 701-702. Nummorum autem tanta fuit carentia et raritas, quod si etiam summa frumenti levi pretio venundaretur, emptorem vix inveniret sufficientem. For the actual prices, cf. Dunst., p. 208. Taxster, *apud* B. Cotton, p. 137. Fabyan, p. 343. Rish., Chronicon, notes, pp. 112-114. Also Mat. Par., as cited *supra*.

CHAPTER III

THE OUTBREAK: AND THE CULMINATION OF THE NATIONAL MOVEMENT

PART I

THE REFORM PARLIAMENTS OF THE YEAR 1258

IN the year 1257 it was calculated by an actual computation that the king had spent 950,000 marks since his days of spoliation and wastefulness began — an immense sum, whose method of expenditure had rather injured, than profited, the kingdom.[1] Henry's shameful alliance with the papacy had resulted in draining England of its wealth, in turning Henry himself from the pursuit of national objects for the sake of a fictitious greatness on the continent, and, through the intrusion of foreigners into bishoprics and benefices, in debasing and partially denationalizing the English church. As an indirect result of the impoverishment of the kingdom, and as the direct result of Henry's denationalizing policy, which had consistently favoured aliens in church and state at

---

[1] Mat. Par., V., p. 627.

the expense of his English subjects, the military vigour of the nation had been sapped — as the Welsh war had demonstrated. Seemingly, never since the days in which the barons had invoked Louis' aid against John had the liberties of the English nation been at a lower ebb. A contemporary chronicler[1] draws a pitiful picture of England's extremity: "So many aliens of divers tongues had already multiplied for many years in England, and had been so enriched with revenues, lands, towns, and other property, that they held the English in the greatest contempt as an inferior race. There were indeed some who said — knowing their secrets — that if their power should increase, they would destroy all the nobles of the land by poison,[2] dethrone the king, and thus at length subdue all England to their sway forever. Moreover, four of the king's brothers — Æthelmar, bishop-elect of Winchester, William of Valence, Guy and Geoffrey of Lusignan, — exalted above the other aliens by dignities and riches beyond measure, raged against the English with intolerable pride, afflicting them cruelly with many injuries of various kinds. Nor did any one dare to oppose their presumptuous acts through fear of the king.[3] Yet not only these, but also Englishmen, kin-

---

[1] Ann. Wav., pp. 349, 350.

[2] Cf. Mat. Par., V., pp. 705, 707. Nearly all the chroniclers accuse the Poitevins of being poisoners. Reports need not be true to arouse popular indignation.

[3] Rish., Chronicon, pp. 3, 7. Mat. Par., V., pp. 594, 708, 738, 739; VI., pp. 400–409. Rymer, I., p. 373. Si quis contra ipsos (fratres regis) vel eorum alterum deferret in judicio quæstionem, Rex . . .

dled by the fire of avarice, rose against Englishmen,[1] the greater against the smaller; and they strove by lawsuits and fines, by tallages, exactions, and various wrongs, to take from every man his property. The laws and ancient customs were decayed or nullified completely; each man did what was right in his own eyes, and nowhere, except for money, could justice be readily procured. Nor can any one enumerate all the evils which at that time were being done in England. At length, in this year (1258), earls and barons, archbishops, bishops, and the other magnates of England — divinely roused from sleep — perceived the wretched prostration of the land, unanimously formed a league, and daringly exhibited lionlike courage and strength." For many years they had been powerless to accomplish any permanent reform: the church had been fettered by its allegiance to the pope, by the oppression of the royal power in alliance with the papal, and by the inner discord and weakness engendered by the presence of aliens in all ecclesiastical offices, from the archbishopric of Canterbury down to the humblest prebend with a salary attached: the barons, on the other hand, although they had bravely opposed both royal and papal encroachments, had been for the most part deprived of efficient aid from the clergy, and, above all, had

---

contra conquerentem mirabiliter turbabatur; et cui judex debebat esse propitius, ad corum suggestionem fiebat adversarius, et nonnunquam terribilis inimicus.

[1] Cf. Mat. Par., V., p. 316. Burt., p. 442. Robert of Gloucester, p. 533.

been torn into factions by mutual jealousies. It had assuredly been on account of no mere fear of pope or king, that the realm had not long ago been freed.[1] The means of binding the king had been too hard to find, and the barons had lacked a leader. But now both the hour and the man had come. The dangers which threatened the very existence of the nation compelled united action on the part of its defenders, and the temper of the nation had been at length roused to such a point that drastic measures would be not only proposed, but enforced, if need be, at the point of the sword. The postponement of the reform had rendered its accomplishment certain, provided that success itself did not, as in the case of the Great Charter,[2] bring disunion in its train. And so it came to pass that in a series of assemblies between the first week of April,[3] 1258, and the middle of the following July, stringent measures for the welfare of the land were adopted and so far enforced that the land was rid of the aliens.

The first of these parliaments met at London. The immediate topics for consideration were the Welsh war and the Sicilian enterprise, but the stormy discussion of these themes, and the abuses connected with them, led to the far more important subject of constitutional reform.

---

[1] Cf. Rish., Chronicon, p. 7. Quia, Romanorum extollentiam humiliando, curiam Romanam offenderent, tum quia regni statum et consuetudinas meliorando, et fratrum regis elata cornua constringendo, regiam indignationem in se ipsos provocarent.

[2] *Vide* Stubbs' Const. Hist., II., pp. 2, 3.

[3] The exact day is uncertain. Mat. Par., V., p. 676. Post diem Martis, quæ vulgariter Hokedai appellatur, = after April 2d.

In March, the Welsh had formed with certain magnates of Scotland a commercial treaty and a league of offence and defence.[1] Moreover, with boasts that they had not only beaten off the royal armies with heavy loss but had also conquered the whole nobility of England, they had recently invaded the county of Pembroke with fire and sword. The danger was so urgent that even William de Valence was moved to complain — presumably, however, rather from regard to his lordship of Pembroke than from any desire to benefit the realm at large. Henry's answer to William at least was easy: "Then, dearest brother, expend your abundant treasures to avenge us." But after asserting in general terms that the successes of the Welsh were due to the consent and help of English traitors, William descended to specific accusations. Attacking Leicester openly, in the presence of the king and many nobles, he called him an old traitor and liar. The earl angrily rejoined, "No, no, William, I am no traitor nor the son of a traitor; our fathers were by no means alike." Undoubtedly blood would have been shed, had not the king himself stepped between them.[2] However, after several days' debate, the Welsh question was disposed of by a general summons to assemble for the campaign at Chester on the 17th of June, with horses and arms.[3]

The more delicate task remained to be accomplished. The coming of Herlot, who, although not a legate, af-

---

[1] Rymer, I., p. 370.
[2] Mat. Par., V., pp. 676, 677. De Valence included Gloucester in the specific charge of treachery.   [3] *Ibid.*, p. 677.

fected all a legate's pomp and received from Henry the welcome of a legate,[1] had been the chief cause for the holding of the parliament. In the pope's name he now demanded from the king a sum of money so large that it "caused the ears of the hearers to tingle,"[2] involving, as was said,[3] one-third of all the property, both real and personal, in England. The barons loudly complained. They could no longer pour out their "substantiolas" except to their own irremediable destruction. Through his own folly, unwisely and improperly, without deliberation or the advice of his nobles, Henry had sought the acquisition of Sicily. Richard of Cornwall, a wiser man than he, had refused the same crown because of the inaccessibility of the country and his fear of Roman intrigue and Sicilian treachery. Yet by shrewdly demanding terms which he knew that the pope would refuse to grant, he had nevertheless succeeded in retaining papal favour. Henry, on the other hand, lured by a shadowy promise, had accepted the crown for Edmund, given all that he had to the pope, promised more, and opened up the way to papal extortion.[4] Then, passing to more general topics of complaint, the barons reproached the king for non-

---

[1] Mat. Par., V., p. 673.   [2] *Ibid.*, p. 676.
[3] Theok., p. 163. Cf. Dunst., p. 208. Centum milia marcarum et amplius.
[4] Mat. Par., V., pp. 680, 681. Cf. Rymer, I., p. 302. For assumption of the business without the barons' consent, cf. Rymer, I., p. 373. Noster rex, absque nostro consilio et assensu, immo nobis reclamantibus et invitis, hoc negotium assumpsisset. The royalist Wykes says, p. 126, Rex autem minus provide negotio se immiscuit.

observance of his promises to the church and for the violation of the Charters which he had so frequently confirmed for money. Contrary to the laws and customs of the realm he had placed his half-brothers, though aliens, in positions of the greatest influence,[1] nor did he allow any writ to go out from his chancery[2] against them, although their own arrogance and the abuses of their bailiffs were notorious. Simon de Montfort then inveighed against the presumption of the aliens and of William de Valence in particular, demanding instant justice. His appeal, significantly enough, was directed not to the king, but to the general body of peers.[3] That the king had enriched foreigners at the expense of his natural subjects and to the subversion of the realm, did not fail to be mentioned. Especial importance was attached to the fact — itself an incitement to remedy abuses by the strong hand — that the king's power was too weak to enforce the laws of the land or to check the incursions of the Welsh, an enemy universally despised. The natural conclusion was that the excesses of the king demanded exceptional treatment.[4] Herlot was told that Henry did not have so much money, and could not have it. When he threatened to excommunicate the king and all the magnates, saying that the king had bound them and their lands in pay-

---

[1] Cf. Rish., Chronicon, p. 3. Consiliarii, præ omnibus indigenis et naturalibus regni, secretiores ac specialiores.

[2] Cf. the remarkable passage in Mat. Par., V., p. 594. Also Oxenedes, p. 225.

[3] Mat. Par., V., p. 689. Non tamen regi, sed universitati.

[4] *Ibid.* Excessus regis tractatus exigit speciales.

ment of their claim, both laymen and clergy indignantly responded that they were free men, and it was therefore beyond the king's power so to bind them.[1] Finally, on the 30th of April, the magnates delivered their ultimatum to the king.

At three o'clock in the afternoon, earls, barons, and knights, all in their military dress and wearing their swords, repaired to the royal hall at Westminster. Leaving their weapons at the entrance, however, they advanced to salute the king with all due respect and deference. In a voice shaking with fear, Henry asked if they meant to take him captive, and what was their will. The barons at once disclaimed any hostile intention, but through their spokesman, Roger Bigod, proceeded to demand the immediate expulsion of the Poitevins, the appointment of twenty-four of the wisest men of England as a council whose advice the king and Edward should be bound by oath to follow, and the delivery of the great seal to whomsoever the twenty-four should name as chancellor. This mode of procedure, said Bigod, would redound to the honour and profit of the whole realm, and would release the king from his troubles. It had been unanimously adopted by the baronage.[2] On that very day [3] Henry yielded; and on the 2d of May he published letters-patent [4] whose nature

---

[1] Dunst., p. 208. Mat. Par., V., p. 682.
[2] Theok., pp. 163, 164. Wisest men — videlicet, episc., comitum, baronum, electorum. Mat. Par., V., p. 682. Quasi uno ore.
[3] Theok., p. 164.
[4] Sel. Chart., pp. 380, 381. Rymer, I., pp. 370, 371.

was such as to ensure a speedy reform. After reciting the summons to the parliament and the character of the business there to be transacted, the document continues: "And since the magnates promised that if we would cause the state of the kingdom to be rectified by a council of our faithful subjects, and if the pope would so mitigate the conditions for the acquirement of Sicily that the business could be prosecuted with success, they would themselves faithfully labour to obtain a general aid from the commonalty of the kingdom for this purpose; we have therefore granted to them that, before next Christmas, we will reform the state of our kingdom by the advice of worthy and faithful men of our realm of England, together with the counsel of a papal legate, — if one shall have entered in the meantime, — and this reform we will firmly maintain and observe." The king next promises to be bound by ecclesiastical censure in case he violates his covenant, and rehearses Edward's consent to the foregoing.[1] The document was signed by many of the aliens, in the presence of a large number of the nobility. By another letter-patent[2] of the same date, the execution of the reform was placed in the hands of twenty-four men, twelve to be nominated by the king and twelve by the barons. To their decrees the king and Edward swore to submit. Soon afterward, the parliament was adjourned to meet at Oxford on the 11th of June, when the reformatory measures were to be perfected.

---

[1] Edward gave his consent reluctantly. Theok., p. 164.
[2] Sel. Chart., p. 381. Rymer, I., p. 371.

Incredible as it may seem, Henry had not refrained even during this critical period from his wonted prodigality and extortion. With a war before him whose expenses he was too poor to defray, he yet found means to present 1000 marks to Thomas of Savoy and £200 to the Poitevin William de Saint Hermete, his favourite carver. The former received rich gifts also from the queen, and at once crossed the Channel to continue with English gold his war with Turin.[1]

In the face of the barons' daily censure for his illegal exactions, and rendered desperate by their refusal to grant him money, Henry had recourse to a system of extortion from individual churchmen which well illustrates his own shifty dealings, the character and methods of his agents, and the burdens which he imposed on the church. The king first induced Richard, the abbot of Westminster, to become his surety to the amount of 2500 marks, and thus obtained a leverage for his proposed exactions. He then sent Simon Passelew, a degenerate Englishman, to other abbeys on a similar errand. Coming first to Waltham, he showed the royal order and the abbot of Westminster's acceptance, and demanded a similar compliance. The abbot replied that the abbey was not only unwilling to bind itself to the payment of money, but by the Decretals[2] was even positively forbidden to do so. To

---

[1] Mat. Par., V., pp. 678, 702.

[2] Decret. III., tit. 23. De solutionibus. Firmiter inhibemus ne quis præsumat ecclesiam sibi commissam pro alienis gravare debitis

Simon's assurance that Henry would give ample security, he rejoined that he had no wish to oppose the king in a lawsuit, for they could not contend on equal terms. So after Simon had had recourse to threats, but in vain, he angrily took his way to St. Albans. Thither the abbot of Waltham had already despatched swift and secret messengers to give warning. Simon, asserting that he had just come from London after an all-night's ride, dozed for a moment before entering the abbot's presence, and then, opening the business as before, proceeded at once to threats. The abbot in reply said that he could not assent, for it would be iniquitous and contrary to papal prohibition. He then produced a bull addressed to abbot Garinus and his successors, commanding them under penalty of suspension and interdict to bind their abbey in no wise. Only then was the full extent of the king's duplicity revealed. Simon replied that the abbot's anxiety was groundless, for brother Mansuetus was now at court, sent by the pope at the king's request, and clothed with full powers expressly to absolve and free from their ecclesiastical obligations all men who were disposed to help the king in this great emergency.[1] To clinch the argument, he added that in case of a further refusal he should return at once to London to report the abbot's contumacy and contempt for the office and power of Mansuetus. The abbot persisting in his denial, Simon shifted his ground.

---

aut litteras alicui seu sigilla concedere, quibus possent ecclesiæ obligari. Cited by Luard, Mat. Par., V., p. 683.

[1] Mat. Par., V., pp. 679, 685, 686.

It would be his own ruin with the king, if he returned unsuccessful; and besides, the whole wealth of the abbey was the gift of the king or of his predecessors, whence it was the abbot's bounden duty to come to the king's assistance. The first plea could have but little weight: to the second, the answer was given: "All things belong to the king for protection, not for destruction. To this the king swore in his coronation-oath and frequently since. We will therefore not yield to your wicked suggestions." In sheer despair, Simon then resorted to his last wile, requesting the abbot to draw up documents such as the king desired, seal them, and deposit them in his own treasury, so that if his heart softened, the king might readily obtain them. Said the abbot, "We will not set an evil example to others," and so, confounded, the tempter withdrew. Foiled here, he proceeded to Reading, — not to London as he had said, — but the sturdy monks, "forewarned, withstood him manfully," and the king failed of his purpose.[1] It was largely on account of this failure that the king on the 30th of April had humiliated himself before the barons, and confessing that he had been misled too frequently by evil counsel,[2] took for almost the first time in a quarter of a century a step in the direction of a genuine reform.

During the five weeks which elapsed before parliament reassembled, neither clergy nor baronage were idle. The latter, indeed, had demanded the adjourn-

---

[1] Mat. Par., V., pp. 682-688.   [2] *Ibid.*, p. 689.

ment, because from old experience they knew the king's faithlessness and the consequent need and excessive difficulty of "finding a knot with which to bind their Proteus."[1] The great earls of Gloucester, Leicester, Hereford, the Earl Marshall, and many other nobles therefore entered into a solemn league, and consolidated their power in order to withstand the assaults at once of the king and the aliens.[2]

As early as the 19th of April, Archbishop Boniface, at Herlot's[3] instance — for Herlot had been sent not only "to reform the Sicilian business," but incidentally to wring money from the clergy — had summoned a convocation[4] to meet at Merton on the Tuesday before June 11th. The primary cause of the meeting was the consideration of the papal demands, — especially for a tallage of three marks levied by Herlot on every religious body throughout England,[5] — but the opportunity for complaining of the king's oppression of the church seems to have been eagerly embraced. No doubt the recent action of the baronage, so acceptable to the great body of the clergy, had proved stimulating; their action, at any rate, at this convocation was in perfect accord with the baronial spirit, although the reforms proposed were foredoomed to a paper existence.[6] The preamble

---

[1] Mat. Par., V., p. 494.

[2] *Ibid.*, V., pp. 689, 690. Rish., Chronicon, p. 8.

[3] Rymer, I., pp. 358, 366. Burt., pp. 409-411. Theok., p. 163. Dunst., p. 208. Mat. Par., V., p. 676.

[4] Burt., pp. 411, 412. Theok., p. 163. "Parum ante." Date was June 6th. [5] Burt., p. 411.

[6] Theok., p. 163. Et de oppressione, sed nihil profecti sunt.

vigorously states that the church was oppressed contrary to divine law, canon law, and the liberties guaranteed by royal charter, and therefore its walls, sapped by the engines of the temporal power, must be repaired forthwith. The most significant article in the document is the order that any person guilty of wasting the property of churches, while vacant, shall be excommunicated without delay — even the king himself.[1] This struck at the fountain-head. The assembly also put on record the gravamina [2] formerly engrossed by the great bishop of Lincoln, indubitably proving that his spirit was still abroad in the land.

The Mad Parliament

By his consent to the project of reform, and to the election of the twenty-four who were to reconstruct the state of the realm " ad honorem Dei et ad fidem nostram ac regni nostri utilitatem," as well as by his oath to maintain and observe their ordinances,[3] the king had given full play to the forces which for twenty-five years had been baffled by his obstinacy and double-dealing, and chafing under the sense of their own impotence. Under the circumstances, moderation could scarcely be expected, nor could a constitution, perfect in all its details, be expected to result from the labours of two hostile political groups, — especially since the reformers

---

[1] Burt., pp. 412–422. Special article is found on p. 420.
[2] Burt., pp. 422–425.
[3] Sel. Chart., p. 381. Rymer, I., p. 371.

were themselves men who had only recently buried mutual jealousies, whose moral standards were exceedingly dissimilar, and whose strongest bond of union was the common danger and the sense of nationality. Those reforms, to be sure, upon which the baronial party were heartily agreed — viz., the preservation of English nationality and constitutional freedom by means of the expulsion of alien elements from the commonwealth — were certain to be thoroughly carried out: it was equally certain, however, that all measures which involved theory rather than practice would meet with opposition from some quarter, and remain either untouched or imperfect. In other words, the temporary work of destruction would in the main be well done; the permanent reform of the constitution — a work which demanded the finest constructive statesmanship — would be of very dubious success. The truth of this was proved by the sequel.

On the 11th of June the barons assembled at Oxford to begin their arduous task. Profoundly distrusting the king's intentions, and fearing the intrigues of the aliens, they availed themselves of the summons to the Welsh war as a pretext for appearing fully armed and accompanied by large bodies of retainers.[1] As an extra precaution they ordered the seaports to be guarded.[2] A petition for the redress of grievances had been drawn

---

[1] Mat. Par., V., pp. 690, 696. Burt., p. 438. Rish., Chronicon, p. 8. According to one writer, sixty thousand persons assembled. Rish., Chronicon, notes, p. 114.

[2] Mat. Par., V., p. 696.

up, and this was now presented.[1] It contained twenty-nine articles, all of undoubted justice, and all rehearsing violations of the principles contained in the Great Charter. By far the major part refer to various encroachments of the royal power upon the rights of mesne lords, to abuses practised by itinerant justices, sheriffs, and royal purveyors, to violations of the forest charters, of the law of escheat, and of patronage-rights in the case of abbeys of private foundation, and to the impoverishment of the land by Christian usurers who were not subject to tallage, and by Jews in league with the powerful.[2] Most important of all, as illustrating the very real perils which threatened English national independence, are the fourth, fifth, sixth, and fifteenth articles. The first of these requests that "the king's castles be committed to the guardianship of loyal men of English birth, on account of the many emergencies which might arise in England;" the second requests particularly that such "royal castles as are situated on the sea-coast, where boats can land, be committed to faithful men of English birth on account of the very many and evident perils which may arise if they are entrusted to others." The third relates to the marriage of the king's female wards, requesting that "they should not be married with disparagement — *that is, to men who are not of the English nationality.*" The last is, if possible, still more significant: "Likewise the barons ask that no one be permitted to fortify a castle at a sea-

---

[1] Sel. Chart., pp. 382–387. Burt., pp. 439–443.
[2] Cf. Stubbs' Const. Hist., II., pp. 76, 77.

port or on a neighbouring island, except by the consent of the council of the whole realm of England, because many dangers may thence arise." Nearly all the royal castles were at this time in the hand of aliens.[1]

Before these abuses could be redressed, the constitutional machinery had to be constructed. Arrangements had been made already for the appointment of the committee of twenty-four; the members were now named,[2] and after the king and the reluctant Edward had sworn to accept and observe their provisions,[3] they entered at once upon their duties. It is unnecessary here to discuss at length the curiously intricate and somewhat primitive methods[4] which their mode of procedure involved and which marked its tentative character. Their measures were to be of two kinds: first, the formation of a permanent constitution, involving the appointment of permanent officials and the regulation of their powers and duties; second, the construction of temporary machinery to deal with current questions — the redress of grievances of all kinds, and the aid which the barons had promised provisionally for the war.

Very early in the parliament the twenty-four had

---

[1] Burt., pp. 443, 444. Litera cujusdam de curia regis de parliamento Oxoniæ.

[2] Shirley, II., pp. 127, 128. For their names, *vide* Burt., p. 447; Pauli, Gesch. von Eng., III., p. 717, n. 2; Stubbs' Const. Hist., II., pp. 77, 78, 85. The last-mentioned page contains a very useful table.

[3] Rymer, I., p. 373. Burt., p. 457. Theok., p. 164. Wykes, p. 119. Osney, pp. 118, 119. Rish., Chronicon, p. 3.

[4] *Vide* Stubbs' Const. Hist., II., pp. 77, 78, n. 4. Pauli, Gesch. von Eng., III., pp. 716–718.

appointed Hugh Bigod justiciar,[1] and by a system of cross selection the twelve who represented the king's interest[2] had named two of the opposing twelve, who in turn had nominated two of the royalist twelve, to act conjointly[3] in the nomination of a permanent council of fifteen. This body was empowered "to advise the king in good faith concerning the government of the realm and all things which appertained to the king or to the kingdom; and to amend and redress all things which they shall see require to be redressed and amended. And over the chief justice and over all the people. And if they cannot all be present, that which the majority shall do shall be firm and established."[4] This council was to be confirmed by the twenty-four. As finally constituted, it contained ten of the baronial and but five of the royal party.[5]

In order to ensure the due hearing and redress of future grievances, it was next provided that a parliament should meet three times a year — on the octave[6] of St. Michael, on the morrow[7] of Candlemas, and on the 1st of June. This parliament was to consist of

---

[1] Burt., p. 443. Mat. Par., V., p. 698. Wykes, p. 120. Osney, p. 119.

[2] Rymer, I., p. 371. Sel. Chart., p. 381. Per XII fideles de concilio nostro jam electos et per alios XII fideles nostros, electos ex parte procerum ipsorum. Shirley, II., pp. 127, 128. June 26, 1258.

[3] Burt., p. 449. Sel. Chart., p. 389.

[4] Burt., pp. 453, 505.

[5] For names, *vide* Burt., p. 449. Cf. Pauli, Gesch. von Eng., III., pp. 717, 718. The royal order for the election of the fifteen is dated June 26, 1258. Shirley, II., pp. 127, 128.

[6] October 6th.   [7] February 3d.

the permanent council of fifteen plus twelve others elected by the barons in behalf of the entire commonalty of the whole land. It was to assemble whether specially summoned or not, and provision was made for its summons on extraordinary occasions by royal writ. Whatever the parliament decreed was to bind the commonalty. The object to be attained by limiting the membership to so few was stated to be the saving of cost to the community.[1] It served, however, to deepen the oligarchical character of the whole scheme and to ensure its ultimate insufficiency.

The next step was to provide for the faithful discharge of the duties of the higher officials. To this end the tenure of office was limited to one year in the case of the three great officials and of the sheriffs. At the end of each year examination of accounts and conduct was to be made before the king, the council, and the official's successor. Reappointment was not definitely forbidden, however. The duties of all officials were clearly stated, and a stringent oath of faithful performance was exacted. The justiciar was sworn to act in all cases for the profit of the king and kingdom, according to the provisions of the twenty-four and by the counsel of the king and his magnates. The chancellor was sworn to seal no writs, except writs of course, without the commandment of the king and council, and to seal nothing contrary to the provisions of the twenty-four. Gifts of a great wardship or es-

---

[1] Sel. Chart., pp. 390, 392, 394, 396. Burt., pp. 449, 452, 502, 504.

cheats required the formal assent of the great council, or of the major part. The treasurer's accounts were to be audited yearly, and posts at the treasury were to be filled by the nominees of the twenty-four. "To the treasury all issues of the land should come, and no part elsewhere."[1] In these words the king's misuse of the finances received decisive check.

It is unfortunate that the method of the appointment of the great officials is not definitely stated; it was probably the result of a compromise, for although Hugh Bigod, at this time a member of the baronial party, had been made justiciar at once, the great seal still remained in the hands of the king's nominee. Then, too, Philip Lovel, a royal favourite, retained the headship of the treasury until October, when, in consequence of depredations on the royal game-preserves, he lost both the royal favour and his place. The barons, mainly at the instance of the justiciar, then appointed John of Crakehall in his stead, at the same time making sweeping changes at the exchequer. In this way the late scene of riotous prodigality was transformed.[2]

This, together with the reconfirmation of the Charters,[3] completed the permanent constitution as established by the twenty-four. Meanwhile, other ordinances of scarcely less moment had been passed by them for

---

[1] Burt., pp. 448, 450, 451. Dunst., pp. 209, 210. Sel. Chart., pp. 389, 390, 391. E la vengent totes les issues de la tere, et en nule part ailurs.

[2] Mat. Par., V., pp. 714, 715, 719, 720. Dunst., p. 210. Cf. Stubbs' Const. Hist., II., p. 80.

[3] Burt., pp. 452, 504. Sel. Chart., pp. 391, 395.

the regulation of current affairs. The amendment of the state of the church was committed to the original twenty-four, "when they shall see place and time."[1] Another special body of twenty-four was elected by the barons to treat of the aid for the king.[2] The importance of the cities received the following recognition:[3] "Be it remembered to amend the exchange of London, and the city of London, and all the other cities of the king which have gone to shame and destruction by the tallages and other oppressions." And first of all in the order of time,[4] and certainly not last in importance, provision had been made for the custody of the royal castles. These had been, as a general rule, in the hands of aliens;[5] they were now entrusted to sure men of English birth, sworn to keep them loyally and in good faith, for the use of the king and his heirs, and to give them up only to the king and his heirs, and that by the written order of the royal council. This provision was to be binding for twelve years only.[6] A second ordinance [7] of kindred nature provided that in view of the king's poverty, and the grave perils which would consequently ensue if the realm should be attacked by a foreign power,[8] all lands, holdings, and castles which

---

[1] Burt., p. 450. Sel. Chart., p. 390.
[2] Burt., p. 450. Sel. Chart., p. 390.
[3] Burt., pp. 452, 504. Sel. Chart., pp. 392, 395.
[4] Immediately after the justiciar's appointment. Burt., p. 443.
[5] Burt., pp. 443, 444. Blaauw, Barons' War, p. 57, n. 2, enumerates fifteen.
[6] Burt., pp. 443, 444, 448, 449, 453. Sel. Chart., pp. 389, 392, 393.
[7] Burt., p. 444.
[8] Peace was made with Wales June 17, 1258. Rymer, I., p. 372.

had been alienated by the king should be restored forthwith.

Although the Poitevins, as well as the king, Edward, and the English barons, had sworn to accept the reforms decreed by the council of twenty-four, the first named had none the less tried with all their power, exercising undue influence particularly upon the prince, to prevent the council from accomplishing its task.[1] When, therefore, the king on the 22d of June[2] took the decisive step of issuing a writ requiring the surrender of the royal castles, the Poitevins flatly refused to comply. A stormy scene ensued. Simon de Montfort, in prompt obedience to the king's command, had already surrendered his two castles of Odiham and Kenilworth. It must have afforded the proud earl rare satisfaction to be able from his vantage-ground of constitutional authority to say to the obstreperous William de Valence, "Be sure that we will have the castles or your head" — a saying to which the rest assented.[3] Henry d'Almayne, son of Richard of Cornwall, also refusing to swear to this provision on the ground that he had no land except at his father's will, that he could therefore take no oath without his father's permission, and besides was not a peer, the baronage returned the answer that if he did not swear, he should never obtain one furrow of land in England. They then granted

---

[1] Rymer, I., p. 373. Burt., p. 448. Sel. Chart., p. 388. Mat. Par., V., pp. 696, 697.

[2] 42 Pat. 6. *Vide* Pauli, Gesch. von Eng., III., p. 720, n. 1.

[3] Mat. Par., V., pp. 697, 698.

him a respite of forty days in which to consult his father.[1]

At the opening of the parliament the twenty-four had sworn a most solemn oath "not to fail for gift nor for promise, for love nor for hate, nor for fear of any one, nor for gain, nor for loss, loyally to do according to the tenor of the letter which the king and his son have together given" for the reformation of the realm.[2] According to Matthew Paris the barons now renewed[3] their oath at a meeting in the house of the Fratres Prædicatores, vowing never to be turned from their purpose of ridding the land of the aliens and of enacting praiseworthy laws. All who refused to join them should be compelled to do so, or be considered mortal enemies.[4]

After de Montfort's speech to de Valence, the aliens, together with John of Warenne whom they seem to have overpersuaded, perceived that it was necessary to seek refuge in flight. Leaving Oxford secretly while the noonday meal was preparing, they spurred to Winchester, there to seek refuge in the castle of Wolvesham, under the fostering care of Bishop Æthelmar. In guilty terror they cast frequent looks behind them as they fled, and caused their followers to mount high watch-towers

---

[1] Burt., p. 444. Mat. Par., V., p. 697.
[2] Burt., p. 448. Sel. Chart., p. 393. Mat. Par., V., p. 696.
[3] Mat. Par., V., p. 697.
[4] Mat. Par., V., p. 697. Dunst., p. 209. Wykes, pp. 119, 120. Rish., Chronicon, p. 8. Quod utique omnium baronum fixum erat propositum ut eos . . . ab Anglia expellerent, et sic compendiosius de negociis regni tractarent et disponerent. Rish., Chronica, pp. 2, 3. Non tamen omnes, sed præcipue Pictavenses, — a convincing example of the fusion of the constitutional and national movements.

to see if perchance the barons were already in pursuit.¹ They were true Ishmaelites; even the queen had turned against them.²

Perceiving the full gravity of the situation, the barons had already ordered that the seaports should be still more strictly guarded, and that London gates should be barred at night.

> Per noctes portæ clauduntur Londoniarum
> Mœnia ne forte fraus frangat Francigenarum

ran an epigram of the time.³ Without delay the king and the barons proceeded with horses and arms to Winchester, resolved to prevent any importation of alien troops and to give the land quiet. And thus, says Matthew Paris, the Oxford parliament was terminated, an end having been reached, not appointed.⁴ This occurred on the 22d of June, or a little later.⁵ Until the 5th of July⁶ a series of ignominious negotiations⁷

---

[1] Burt., p. 444. Mat. Par., V., pp. 696–698. Theok., p. 165. Rish., Chronicon, p. 8. Dunst., p. 209, says, clam et de nocte . . . recesserunt. Ant. Leg., p. 38.

[2] Mat. Par., V., 703. . . . regina Franciæ . . . de Pictavensibus illis reposuerat querimoniam, quod enormiter scandalizaverant et diffamaverant sororem suam reginam Angliæ. Waverley, p. 355. Hæc quidem provisio imprimis placuit reginæ, dum quidam barbari sibi displicentes Angliæ cogerentur valefacere.

[3] Mat. Par., V., p. 697.   [4] Ibid., p. 698.

[5] The writ demanding the castles was dated on that day, and Matthew's account would lead one to believe that the aliens fled almost at once after de Montfort's speech. Ann. Winton., p. 97, dates the "parliament of Winchester" *circa* July 2d.

[6] Rymer, I., p. 374.

[7] Burt., pp. 444, 445. Rymer, I., p. 373. Rish., Chronicon, pp. 8, 9.

proceeded; John of Warenne made his peace with the baronial party and swore to the provisions *in toto*; but although the Poitevins finally promised a similar compliance, they were told that they were unworthy of credence, and at last, on their refusal to stand trial, were banished from the realm.[1] On the 14th of July[2] the king's half-brothers, together with several foreigners of lesser note, crossed the Straits of Dover. Out of their immense accumulations they bore with them, by permission, only 6000 marks.[3] The rest — except certain large sums which they contrived later to smuggle across — fell to the coffers of the state.[4] And the land had rest from their exactions.[5]

This great victory did not stop the action of the provisional government. No sooner had the disturbing influence of the aliens been removed than Prince Edward, however reluctantly, submitted himself to the barons and received four counsellors whom they placed by his side. The fickle king, passing from one extreme to the other, had frequently asked the barons to station only

---

[1] Burt., p. 445. Mat. Par., V., p. 702. Theok., p. 165. Rish., Chronicon, pp. 8, 9. Dunst., p. 209. Ant. Leg., p. 38. Osney, p. 119.

[2] Safe-conduct, July 5th, Rymer, I., p. 374. Burt., p. 445. Mat. Par., V., p. 702, dates their departure July 18th.

[3] Burt., p. 445. Cf. Lib. de Ant. Leg., p. 38. Quibus vero non fuit permissum ad ducendum secum aliquid de thesauris suis, nisi de tantummodo quantum oportebat eis ad expensas. Also Rymer, I., p. 374.

[4] Rymer, I., p. 377. Mat. Par., V., pp. 704, 713, 730; VI., p. 405. Burt., p. 445. Dunst., p. 209.

[5] Taxster, p. 187; *apud* B. Cotton, p. 137. Quibus expulsis, paulatim prædictæ tortuosæ exactiones cessare cœperunt.

native Englishmen about his person, and this was also done.[1] On the 23d of July, a deputation of the baronage presented themselves before the citizens of London in Guildhall and secured their exceedingly important adherence to the Provisions. To a charter already fortified by the seals of Henry, Edward, and the barons, the city seal was now attached; from this time on, the Provisors held colloquies from day to day, frequently at the New Temple, reforming the uses and customs of the realm.[2] On the 28th of July, Henry, in compliance with the Provisions, issued a general writ to all the sheriffs to inquire by the recognition of four discreet men of each county into the abuses and excesses there committed in times past.[3] A sealed report was to be delivered by the sheriff in person to the council at the opening of the October parliament. The moral effect of this measure must have been very great, for it promised earnestness and better times.

Another procedure[4] was designed to secure the cordial support of the lower clergy. Mindful of the financial and spiritual injuries which had been inflicted upon the realm by the foreigners who had been forced into English benefices by the pope and the king — especially to the pecuniary loss of the lower clergy, who were thus deprived of many valuable livings — the

---

[1] Burt., p. 445. Edward's four were John de Balliol, John de Grey, Stephen Longespée, and Roger de Montalt.

[2] Ant. Leg., pp. 38, 39. Mat. Par., V., p. 704. "In festo Mariæ Magdalenæ," July 22d.

[3] Burt., pp. 446, 456. Sel. Chart., p. 387. Mat. Par., V., p. 714.

[4] Rish., Chronicon, pp. 9, 10.

barons ordered that the revenues due to Italian priests should not be delivered to the aliens, but instead to procurators appointed by the barons. Bishops were in like manner commanded not to defend the foreigners by ecclesiastical censure, nor to interfere in any way for their protection. The very language as well as the spirit of this measure, forcibly recalls the fierce outburst of national enthusiasm in the Twenge riots of twenty-seven years before.[1] For three years the excesses of the pope were stopped.

On the 4th of August, Henry issued letters-patent announcing his intention to be bound by the decisions of the permanent council of fifteen, and requiring his subjects, both clerical and lay, to render them implicit obedience.[2] If anything more could possibly be wanting to establish irrefragably the lawful position of the twenty-four, and the constitutionality of their decrees, it was furnished on the 18th of October. The Provisions of Oxford were published[3] then for the first time officially, and the king signified his adherence to them in a document[4] which enjoys the unique honour of being the first state-paper in the English language the wording of which is extant. Both the Provisions and the king's adherence to them were published in Latin, French, and English — a remarkable testimony to the

---

[1] Cf. Mat. Par., III., pp. 208 *et seq.* Also *supra*, pp. 90, 91, and n. 4. This order dates between 1258-1263.

[2] Shirley, II., p. 129.

[3] The formal publication had been delayed by Gloucester's illness, according to Mat. Par., V., pp. 704, 705.

[4] Sel. Chart., pp. 396-398.

still imperfect homogeneity of England, its increasing political solidarity, the growing political importance of the commons, and the anxiety of the barons to have their measures known to all classes of the commonwealth.

The Provisions themselves, unfortunately, do not exist in their original form. They seem to have been five in number, four of which were acceptable to moderate members of both parties.[1] None of them, if judged by the real needs of the times and the king's instability, were of such a character as to justify the opprobrious epithet of "Mad."[2] All the chroniclers agree, however, in considering these Provisions the cause of the later war. The royalist Wykes, while censuring bitterly the establishment of an executive council, nevertheless finds the true cause of war in what he terms the "fifth provision" — viz., that if any one should dare to thwart (contraire) the Provisions, or refuse to keep them, he should be decreed a public enemy.[3] William de Rishanger, an ardent admirer of de Montfort, with a truer political sense qualifies his praise of the whole body of the Provisions by saying that they all would advantage the realm, "provided they be observed firmly and inviolably by each and all;" he then attributes the immediate cause of war to the same article which Wykes mentions.[4] As a matter of fact, if there had been no Provisions in the year 1258, a rebellion must have taken their place; the fundamental causes of the later war were essentially the same as the causes of the

---

[1] Wykes, p. 119.   [2] Ant. Leg., p. 37.   Illud insane Parliamentum.
[3] Wykes, pp. 119, 120.   [4] Rish., Chronicon, pp. 2, 3.

assembling of the June parliament — manifold violations of national and constitutional rights; the immediate occasion was the attempted limitation of the royal power by a standing committee. This was a provision to which no mediæval king would peaceably submit. The fifth article was but its corollary — a token that the barons were in earnest.

The general results of the Provisions are thus summed up by Daniel,[1] a writer of the early seventeenth century: "Wherein we see what effects it wrought, how no side got but misery and vexation; whilst the one struggled to doe more than it should, and the other to doe lesse than it ought, they both had the worst, according to the usual events of such embroylements." The primary causes of the war amply justified it; the conduct of that wing of the baronial party which was under de Clare's leadership immeasurably weakened the moral strength of the baronial claims; the king renewed his intrigues and demands for irresponsible power under circumstances which gave his cause fictitious strength; and the result was a conflict which would have been ignominious enough for all parties had not the personal character and broad aims of Simon de Montfort lifted the strife far above the pettiness of a mere squabble for the exercise of barren power into the grandeur of an initial contest for the rights of the people.

---

[1] Collection of the Hist. of Eng., p. 155. Cited by Halliwell in the notes to Rish., Chronicon, p. 115. Daniel is published in the first volume of Kennet's Complete Hist. of Eng., 3 vols., folio, 1706.

PART II

THE GOVERNMENT OF THE BARONS: WAR AND PEACE

THE history of England from the October parliament of 1258, at which the barons firmly seized the reins of power by publishing Henry's formal adhesion to the Provisions of Oxford and by installing their nominees in office, is for a considerable period exceedingly intricate.[1] As is usual in such cases, however, there exists an underlying chain of causation whose continuity remains unbroken, and which is itself far more important than any of the details which serve to reveal its existence. The chain now in question was forged by the nature of the rule of the baronial oligarchy, by the unchanged character of king and Roman court, by the steady persistence of the English people and their chosen leader in the struggle for liberty, and by the ferment of political ideas.

The external history of the reign from this time on falls naturally into five divisions. The first extends from October, 1258, to the death[2] of the earl of Glouces-

---

[1] For this period, Shirley's Royal Letters, Vol. II., contains the most recently printed documents; the details in the Preface, pp. viii-xiv, are also very valuable. Pauli, Gesch. von Eng., Vol. III., was printed before these documents were published, and is therefore inadequate between 1260-1263. For the best descriptions of the time, vide Stubbs' Const. Hist., II., pp. 81-93. Pauli, Simon v. Montfort, pp. 94-137. [2] Burt., p. 499.

ter on the 15th of July, 1262; the second embraces the first campaign of the Barons' War, and extends to the Award of Amiens,[1] Jan. 23d, 1264; the third includes the battle of Lewes, and is terminated by the Mise of Lewes,[2] May 15th, 1264; the fourth is the period of Simon's independent rule, and is closed by the battle of Evesham,[3] Aug. 4th, 1265; the fifth and last includes the episode of the Disinherited, and is terminated by the final pacification and the end of the reign. The binding links throughout are continuous constitutional progress and the maintenance of political ideas.

The first period is characterized by the comparatively successful management of foreign affairs [4] by the baronial government as the sworn champions of English nationality, by their failure in domestic rule owing to internal dissensions in the governing body,[5] by the joint

---

[1] Sel. Chart., pp. 406–409. Rymer, I., pp. 433, 434.

[2] Rish., Chronicon, p. 37. Sel. Chart., pp. 334, 335. Wykes, p. 152. *Vide* Blaauw, p. 191.

[3] Rish., Chronicon, p. 47. Lanercost, p. 76. Wykes, pp. 171, 172.

[4] Peace with Wales, Rymer, I., p. 372. June 17, 1258. Cf. Mat. Par., V., p. 727. With Scotland, Rymer, I., pp. 376, 378. With France, on the basis of the surrender of Normandy, Rymer, I., pp. 383, 384, 388–390. Letters to the pope, renouncing Sicily and denouncing Æthelmar, Rymer, I., p. 373. Theok., pp. 170–174. Burt., pp. 457–460. Mat. Par., V., pp. 716, 717; VI., pp. 400–409. For the pope's evasive answer, Mat. Par., VI., pp. 410–416. Blaauw, p. 66, erroneously cites Rymer, I., p. 393, of the date 1260.

[5] Due partly to the cumbrousness of the form of government, divergence of general political views, and mutual jealousies. Gloucester led one wing of the baronial party, Leicester the other. The quarrel broke out in 1259, at the Spring parliament. Mat. Par., V., pp. 737, 744. The immediate cause was probably the Ordinance of March 28, 1259 (Rymer, I., p. 381), which secured to vassals rights corresponding

attempt of pope and king as "lord of the laws"[1] to restore the royal despotism, by frequent arbitrations[2] between the king and the baronage which reached no definite results except to weaken the baronial party and to decentralize its aims, and finally, by the gradual transference of the centre of diplomacy — portentous change — from Rome to France.[3]

---

to those which the king had guaranteed their lords. Cf. Stubbs' Const. Hist., II., p. 82. Differences concerning the French treaty aggravated the quarrel. Cf. Mat. Par., V., p. 745. Wykes, p. 123. Also Rymer, I., pp. 385, 386, 392. The result was that Simon remained much abroad (Mat. Par., V., pp. 732, 737, 744, 745. Mat. West., p. 367. Dunst., p. 217. Osney, p. 129. Rymer, I., p. 409), while Gloucester worked against him with the king. Mat. Par., V., p. 745. Dunst., p. 215 (1260). Dom. rex per falsos accusatores contra com. Simonem iræ suæ fræna relaxavit. Dunst., p. 217 (1261). Inter hæc comes Glov. quasi apostatavit, recedens a consilio Simonis, etc. Cf. Shirley, II., p. 243. For popular ideas of the general discord, *vide* Wright's Pol. Songs, pp. 121-124. Rish., Chronicon, 18-20. This discord, so far as rooted in differences of political aims, was the chief cause of the barons' failure. E.g. Rish., Chronicon, 6. Donec inimico superseminante zizania, etc.

[1] Rymer, I., p. 406. May 7, 1261. "Principes, legum dominos." Bull of Absolution to the Magnates of England.

[2] Arbitrations with the baronage concerning sheriffs, etc., Shirley, II., pp. 192-194, 196, 198. Cf. Pref., pp. xi., xii. Rymer, I., pp. 409, 415. Wykes, p. 130. Rish., Chronica, p. 8. Arbitration with Leicester and France, Shirley, II., pp. 168-171, 173, 174, 242-245. Rymer, I., pp. 416, 418, 422. It was shortly after the cessation of these latter negotiations, which Leicester broke off because "non videbatur . . . quod propter quædam . . . ad honorem suum pacem facere posset his diebus" (Shirley, II., p. 243. Feb. 16, 1263), that war broke out. Gloucester had died in the summer before.

[3] This change was caused largely by the pope's partisanship, — which rendered the arbitration of a legate unwelcome and impossible, — by Leicester's prolonged residence in France, by the French journeys of the king, by the introduction into England of mercenary

The most significant tokens of general discontent and the need of a more comprehensive constitution than was established by either Magna Charta or the Provisions of Oxford were, first, the interposition, in October, 1259, of the unrepresented "Community of the Knighthood of England" in behalf of the execution of the Provisions of Oxford, the performance of baronial promises which had been violated, and the proper observance

---

troops by both parties — Rymer, I., pp. 396, 409; Dunst., p. 214; Shirley, II., pp. 193, 194 — and especially by that clause in the French treaty which enabled the king to purchase mercenaries by means of Louis' payment of money in lieu of five hundred knights to serve Henry for two years — e li Rois d'Angleterre ne doit ces deniers despendre, forsque el servise Deu, ou de l'eglise, ou au profit del roialme d'Angleterre, etc. Rymer, I., pp. 376, 388, 389. October, 1259. The last receipt for this money, significantly enough, is dated May 14, 1264, from the battlefield of Lewes. Rymer, I., p. 440. This change of the diplomatic centre is evidenced (*a*) by frequent references to France as arbitrator in baronial and royal negotiations: (1263) Rish., Chronicon, pp. 14, 15. Ant. Leg., p. 57. Dunst., p. 225. (1264) Award of Amiens; Negotiations at Brackley; Mar. 13, 1264. Rymer, I., pp. 436, 437. Mise of Lewes and negotiations in pursuance thereof. Rish., Chronicon, p. 37. Ant. Leg., p. 63. Shirley, II., pp. 258, 259, 261-264, 274, 276. Rymer, I., pp. 446, 455. Also by the fact that Louis' assent to the Mise of Lewes was demanded. Shirley, II., pp. 257, 258. (*b*) By the fears of indefinite evils which might flow from the king's journeys to France. Rymer, I., pp. 429, 432. Theok., p. 180. Mat. West., p. 378. Rish., Chronica, p. 10. Dunst., p. 218 (1262). Causam itineris fere omnibus cismarinis ignorantibus, et mala inde futura multum pavescentibus. (*c*) By the private negotiations already mentioned between the king and Simon. (*d*) By the stay of the queen in France and the danger of alien invasions. (*e*) By the fact that it was from France, in 1260, that the king committed his first definite breach of the Oxford Provisions, ordering (1) no parliament to be held till his return, Shirley, II., p. 150; (2) resuming the Sicilian affair, Shirley, II., pp. 147, 148.

of the laws; and second, the writ issued jointly by Leicester, Gloucester, and the bishop of Worcester, summoning three knights of each shire to come to St. Albans, *secum tractaturi super communibus negotiis regni*, and the counter-summons[1] of the king. The most important single events of this period — the death of Gloucester excepted — were undoubtedly the acquisition and production of the papal bulls[2] which ab-

---

[1] Burt., p. 471. "Communitas bacheleriæ Angliæ." The summons to the knights included only those "citra Trentam." Sel. Chart., pp. 405, 406. Shirley, II., p. 179. Summons was for Sept. 21, 1261.

[2] After the Provisions of Oxford had been enacted, the pope first showed his readiness to lend assistance by assigning the empire to Richard of Cornwall (Burt., pp. 469, 470. April 30, 1259. Rymer, I., p. 382), by not annulling the Sicilian compact, and by his interposition in favour of Æthelmar of Winchester. Mat. Par., VI., p. 415. Shirley, II., p. 138. Mat. West., p. 377. In flat defiance of the request of the baronial government, Æthelmar was consecrated in May, 1260, but died while on his way to England. Wykes, p. 124. Wav., p. 352. Winton., p. 98. Ant. Leg., p. 49. Dunst., p. 216. Osney, p. 125. Theok., p. 169. Mat. West., pp. 368, 369. Henry gladly accepted the papal overtures, and the result was the first bull of dispensation, Alexander's, April 13, 1261. Rymer, I., p. 405. Produced at Winchester, June 12, 1261. Wykes, p. 128. The second bull, Urban's confirmation, was dated Feb. 25, 1262. Rymer, I., p. 416. It was produced at London, April 23, 1262 (Wykes, p. 130), and published throughout England, May 2, 1262. Rymer, I., p. 419. Ant. Leg., p. 50. For preliminary negotiations, which were difficult, *vide* Rymer, I., pp. 410, 414. Shirley, II. (September, 1261), pp. 188-192, 207-209. Cf. Shirley, II., pp. 104-106. This letter is misplaced by Shirley, under the year 1254. The pope could not be quoted as saying the following words until Normandy had been definitely relinquished by treaty : " Indignanter quæsivit (papa) quare nunc habuistis (sc. Rex Henricus) sigillum majoris magnitudinis *quam tempore quo fuistis dux Normanniæ*, et hoc in opprobrium. Also *vide* the address, from which "dux Normanniæ" is scrupulously omitted. The letter belongs, on its face, to 1261-1262.

solved Henry and the magnates from their oaths to the Provisions, and forbade their observance. The production of the first bull paved the king's way for active measures; the remainder of the year 1261 and the early part of 1262 witnessed the presence in England of rival justiciars and chancellors,[1] and of a double set of sheriffs[2] and aspirants for the custody of royal castles.[3] Both parties had already brought in mercenaries.[4] The two sets of officials clashed, and it seemed that nothing short of a miracle could prevent the clashing of swords as well. But Alexander died, Gloucester deserted his party,[5] Leicester was still entangled in the private French negotiations, and the storm blew over. The production of the second bull brought about a compromise of which Simon disapproved, and which consequently led him to prolong his stay in France.[6] The true significance of the production of the papal bulls is therefore this: it revealed the fixed determination of the king to annul the Provisions of Oxford by fair means or foul, defined the position of the pope with respect to English liberty almost as clearly as in the corresponding case of Magna Charta, and practically presented to the national party the ultimatum, yield or

---

[1] Ant. Leg., p. 49. Mat. West., pp. 380–381. Rish., Chronica, p. 10. Wykes, p. 129. Dunst., p. 217.

[2] Rymer, I., p. 409. Mat. West., pp. 380, 381. Shirley, II., pp. 192, 193.

[3] Rymer, I., pp. 408, 409. Cf. Shirley, II., Pref., p. xi, n. 2. Wykes, pp. 125, 127. Mat. West., p. 379.

[4] Rymer, I., pp. 396, 409. Shirley, II., pp. 193, 194. Dunst., p. 214.

[5] Dunst., p. 217.   [6] Wykes, p. 131.

fight. The answer at first was postponed, but the death of Gloucester, by placing Simon at the head of an undivided party, speedily decided the question in favour of the latter alternative.

The second subdivision of the reign forms the commencement of the Barons' War proper; its immediate causes were the refusal of the young earl of Gloucester[1] to do homage to Edward as commanded by the king,[2] and the refusal of the king to reconfirm and observe the Provisions of Oxford as demanded by Simon on behalf of the barons.[3] The more remote causes, as already stated, were practically the same as the causes of the Mad Parliament of Oxford. The same ideas were still cherished by both parties, and in many respects even the external history of the years antecedent to 1258 had been repeated between 1261 and 1263. This is especially true of the discords in the baronial ranks which had enabled the king to play off one party against the other, the resumption by the king of the old alliance with the pope, the renewal of the Sicilian negotiations,[4] and the unrest of the Welsh border.[5]

---

[1] Dunst., p. 220. He joined Leicester's party, according to Wykes, p. 140, instigante matre sua, blanditiis allectum.

[2] Rymer, I., pp. 425, 427. Ant. Leg., p. 53. Dunst., p. 220.

[3] Dunst., pp. 221, 222.

[4] Rymer, I., p. 405. March, 1261.

[5] July 16, 1259, ratification of the truce with Wales for one year, Rymer, I., p. 387. Concerning reparation for breach of truce, and safe conduct for Welsh envoys, Feb. 25, 1260, Rymer, I., p. 394. Summons to military service against Llewellyn, Aug. 1, 1260, Rymer, I., p. 398. Other measures of the year 1260, Rymer, I., pp. 399, 400. Shirley, II., pp. 156, 157. March 12, 1261, prolongation of truce,

The military operations of this campaign are important not so much from their magnitude, the success achieved by the barons, and the fresh revelation of Simon's oft-praised military skill,[1] as for the manifest determination of the great body of the English people to preserve their ancient and just liberties or to die in their defence. The national character of the war is shown most clearly by the treatment[2] accorded to the

---

Rymer, I., p. 404. 1262, negotiations for a peace, January 8th, Rymer, I., p. 414; June 8th, Rymer, I., p. 420; August 24th and 25th, Shirley, II., pp. 214-217. Rymer, I., p. 421. Complaints of Llewellyn, as dated by Shirley, II., September 26th or 27th, pp. 218, 219. Great outbreak of autumn of 1262, in which the Welsh penetrate to Bergavenny, and which preludes the barons' campaign of 1263, Shirley, II., pp. 219-221. This is the letter which Pauli, III., p. 705, and Rymer, I., p. 339, assign erroneously to 1256. The mention of Basset as justiciar is decisive. Cf. Wykes, 129. Memorandum, quod in Pascha predicta (1261) Dom. Rex, dum fuit apud Wintoniam fecit Cap. Justitiarium de Phil. Basset, etc. For progress of the war, *vide* Shirley, II., pp. 227-233. Rymer, I., pp. 423, 425, 430, 433.

[1] Mailros, pp. 193, 216. Rish., Chronicon, pp. 12, 25, 31, 6: Armorum usu et rei militaris experientia omnibus in suo tempore anteponendus.

[2] Mat. West., p. 383. Rish., Chronicon, pp. 10-12. Rish., Chronica, p. 17. Trivet, pp. 250, 251. Robert of Gloucester, pp. 535-538. Ant. Leg., p. 53. Et semper vexillum Dom. regis coram se detulerunt (barones). Dunst., p. 222. Qui (barones) primo aggressi sunt Petrum episc. Herefordiæ, et ipsum ceperunt, et omnia ejus bona diripuerunt; idem facientes de maneriis Galfridi de Langele et ejus bonis; *nulli ommino malum vel damnum inferentes, nisi alienigenis; et ipsis quia contra statuta Oxoniæ consilium vel auxilium impenderunt,* vel summoniti ad ipsos venire noluerunt; quos omnes juramenti sui transgressores reputabant et felones vocabant; et omnia bona istorum, ubicunque inventa, deprædati sunt, insuper terras et ecclesias alienigenarum, quas feofando et instituendo dederunt. Sed hoc erat contra jura, nec stare potuit. The words in italics are a striking instance of the connection between the national and the constitutional

foreign contemners of the Provisions of Oxford, which to a remarkable degree resembles that of the Twenge riots of thirty-two years before, by the use of the English language as a shibboleth [1] for discovering the enemies of the realm, by the determination at all hazards to obtain the control of the castles and to place the administration of the state in the hands of men of English birth, instincts, and training. The most significant single manifestation of the strength of the desire for national self-government was the offer submitted to the king at London to accept arbitration upon every point at issue, including the complete reconstruction, if necessary, of the Oxford decrees, yet insisting [2] that the administration of the realm be entrusted to native Englishmen. There were no Guelfs or Ghibellines in England to maintain a title blindly for years after its effective meaning had been completely lost; the Provisions of Oxford were no fetish; national freedom was the one longing of the people.

---

movement. Cf. Wykes, pp. 134, 135. It must be remembered that Leicester's party was held responsible by the royalists for the conduct of such free lances as Robert Ferrers, earl of Derby, — iste verbotenus quin pocius fraudulenter consuli (Simoni) adhærens . . . undique deprædando nomine baronum infinita mala perpetravit, parta regis destruxit etiam post pacem clamatam, — and was later imprisoned for treachery. Rish., Chronicon, pp. 20, 21.

[1] Mat. West., p. 383. Tunc erat triste emulis alienigenis videre confusionem eorum. Nam quicumque Anglicum idioma loqui nesciret vilipenderetur a vulgo et despectui haberetur.

[2] Ant. Leg., p. 54. Item petunt quod regnum de cetero per indigenas fideles et utiles sub Dom. Rege gubernetur et non per alios, sicut fit communiter in omnibus aliis mundi regnis.

The two most important political acts of the period were the final acceptance of Louis as an arbitrator, and the formal adhesion[1] of the Londoners for peace or for war, for good or for ill, to the party of Simon de Montfort. The most unmistakable sign of the drift of the times was the growing power of the city communes,[2] especially in London. The day of the popular constitution was now not far distant.

The third period opens with Louis' formal Award at Amiens;[3] this annulled the Provisions of Oxford *in toto* together with the whole body of dependent legislation, stated definitely that the king was free to appoint all officers of state and to install aliens in any position whatever in which he saw fit to employ them, and emphasized the authority of the pope by assigning his earlier cassation of the Provisions as a chief

---

[1] Ant. Leg., pp. 53, 54. About the 24th of June the barons sent the following message to London under Simon's seal: An vellent observare dictas ordinationes et statuta, facta ad honorem Dei, etc., an potius adherere illis qui voluerunt illas infringere. A favourable answer was given later, et ita Barones et Cives sunt confederati, dicentes salva fide Dom. Regis — an empty reservation. League was renewed in 1264 in writing. Ant. Leg., p. 62. The importance of London to the barons is well expressed by the chronicler of Mailros, p. 195. Sine tante civitatis eximio et permaximo auxilio, expulsionem alienorum nullatenus facere potuissent, etc.

[2] Ant. Leg., pp. 55, 61. Winton., p. 101. Communitas Londoniæ, ut dicitur, mira fecit et laude digna. Wykes, p. 138. Ex hac igitur protervia per universum regnum Angliæ consuetudo detestabilis inolevit, quod in omnibus pæne civitatibus et burgis fieret conjuratio ribaldorum qui se bachilarios publice proclamabant.

[3] Ant. Leg., pp. 59–61. Rymer, I., pp. 433, 434. Sel. Chart., pp. 406–409. Shirley, II., pp. 251, 252. Confirmed by Urban, March 16, 1264. Rymer, I., pp. 436–438.

reason [1] for their rejection by himself. The views of the three autocrats would naturally be similar. All rancour, continued the document, was to be laid aside by both parties, and the Award was not to be so interpreted as "to prejudice the royal privileges, charters, statutes, and the laudable customs of the kingdom as they existed before the Oxford Statutes." The Award went much further than was originally intended [2] by at least one of the contracting parties; therefore while it seemed to guarantee the king's final success, it aroused such a storm of discontent that its only important actual effect was to unite all the elements of the opposition more firmly, and to draw party lines more tightly than ever, through the opportunity which it gave to dissidents of withdrawing from the baronial party once for all.[3] It is fruitless here to discuss the question whether Simon's subsequent action in refusing to observe the Award was technically justified or not.[4] That instrument formally recognized the Magna Charta — the basis, as the

---

[1] Maxime cum appareat summum pontificem eas (provisiones) per litteras suas cassas et irritas nunciasse.

[2] Dunst., p. 227. (Rex Franciæ) proprii honoris immemor, et se ultra potestatem sibi concessam extendens. Cf. even the royalist Wykes, p. 139. Forte minus sapienter et utiliter quam deceret eructatione siquidem improvisa suum præcipitavit arbitrium. The barons evidently had not purposed to submit the question of alien castleguards and councillors to Louis of France.

[3] Cf. Rish., Chronicon, pp. 17, 18. Ab hoc tempore factus est novissimus (error) pejor priore. . . . Et (Simon) dixit secretioribus suis, "In multis terris et provinciis diversarum nationum, tam paganorum quam christianorum, extiti: sed in nullis gentibus tantam infidelitatem et deceptionem reppero, quantam in Anglia jam expertus sum." [4] *Vide* Stubbs' Const. Hist., II., p. 92.

national party firmly believed, of the Provisions of Oxford;[1] the Award was self-contradictory[2] and therefore could not be executed to the letter; and at the most it simply caused a recurrence to the state of affairs as it existed on the 10th of June, 1258. If Proteus then needed to be bound, the same necessity still existed, for his nature was unchanged. To all intents and purposes the domestic situation was also the same as at the earlier date. Sicily, indeed, was lost[3] to the king forever, but the vicious alliance with the papacy was more closely knit than ever and was still more directly opposed to the expressed wishes of the nation, while the augmented rage of the people against royal misgovernment in general fully compensated for the friction formerly engendered by the pope's Sicilian demands. The young earl of Gloucester, the city of London, and the Cinq Ports had never submitted to the arbitration and were joined by nearly all the city-communes in England in rejecting it.[4] After Henry had refused the offer of the national party to accept Louis' dictum as it stood, with the single exception of the clause which sanctioned the employment of aliens in

---

[1] Rish., Chronicon, p. 17. Rish., Chronica, p. 12. Wigorn., p. 448.

[2] Wigorn., p. 448. Dicti barones audientes contrarietatem dicti dom. regis . . . dictis suis renunciarunt de plano.

[3] Rymer, I., pp. 428, 429, July 28, 1263. Cf. Raynaldus, 1262, XX. Mansi, T. III., XXII., p. 89.

[4] Ant. Leg., p. 61. Gloucester's name does not appear in the lists of those who subscribed to the arbitration. These lists show clearly the position and adherents of the parties. Shirley, II., p. 252. Rymer, I., pp. 433, 434. Sel. Chart., pp. 406, 407.

the service of the state,[1] the renewal of war was inevitable, and the march of events went steadily on until Henry's power lay shattered on the bloody field of Lewes.

The fourth subdivision is the grand creative era; it was a time of great commotion. All the energies of the skilful politician, warrior, and statesman were tasked to defend himself against attacks from abroad, open enemies at home, and secret traitors. The turning-point of the struggle was the escape[2] of Edward at the Feast of Pentecost from his quasi-confinement at Hereford, and his immediate alliance with the treacherous Gloucester and the Marchers.[3] The end of the great drama was at hand. The capture of the army of the younger Simon at the castle of Kenilworth was but the prelude to the fatal day of Evesham.

Leicester's rule had lasted only fifteen short months. The Charters[4] and the Provisions of Oxford[5] were of course confirmed. The reformation of the state of the

---

[1] Pauli, Simon v. Montfort, p. 133, n. 1. Copie einer Aufzeichnung des Stadtschreibers von London in MS. Mus. Brit., Add. 5444, fol. 66, b. quod saltem unicum et solum remittat articulum, viz. quod alienigenis ab Anglia remotis per indigenas gubernetur, et omnibus statutis provisionibus et ordinationibus regis Franciæ aquiescat. *Vide* also Blaauw, p. 105, n. 1. Henry was then at Oxford and the barons were at Brackley.

[2] Rymer, I., p. 455. Wav., p. 362. Rish., Chronicon, p. 43. Lan., p. 79. Wykes, p. 163. Mail., p. 198. Dunst., p. 239. Rish., Chronica, pp. 33, 34. Nangis, I., p. 228.

[3] Wykes, pp. 164, 165.

[4] Rymer, I., p. 453. Sel. Chart., pp. 416–418.

[5] Rymer, I., p. 453. Wav., pp. 358–361. Ant. Leg., p. 71. Osney, pp. 158, 159.

o

church was entrusted to three elected bishops; their decisions were final, and the secular power was to execute their behests,[1] if summoned to do so. The excellent understanding which existed between the patriotic heads of the church and the practical head of the state was further cemented by the association of the bishop of Chichester with Gloucester and Leicester in the chief executive council,[2] by a decree which made sacrilege a capital offence,[3] and by the grant of a tenth to protect the state from invasion.[4] In strict accordance with the national programme of 1231 and 1263, it was enacted that the revenues of non-resident incumbents and of benefice-holders who had opposed the welfare of the land should be confiscated to the uses of the state.[5] Henceforth, too, the dignitaries as well as the rank and file of the clergy were to obtain their incomes not as a reward for existence but for services rendered. Archbishop Boniface himself was warned that if he re-

---

[1] The bishops were empowered "a purver les choses ke besoignables sont e profitables a plein reformement del estat de saint eglise, a honur Deu, a la foi nostre seinur le Roi, e au profit du reaume. Rymer, I., pp. 443, 444.

[2] Rymer, I., pp. 443, 444.

[3] Rish., Chronica, p. 29. Sed et licet Comes præcepta dedisset, sub pœna decapitationis, ne quis ad sanctam ecclesiam vel cœmeterium deprædaturus intrare præsumeret, nec religiosis viris, vel eorum famulis, manus violentas inferret, nihil hac industria fere profecit.

[4] Rymer, I., p. 445. Rish., Chronicon, p. 36. Ant. Leg., p. 69. Dunst., p. 223. Cf. Wykes, p. 155.

[5] Rymer, I., p. 444. Purveu est ke les bens des benefices de seinte eglise des aliens, e des autres ke ont est *contre la terre*, soient coilli e sauvement garde par les mains des prelaz, descques atant ke soit purveu par comun conseil ke leu devera faire.

mained longer out of England and neglected to provide for the administration of his see, the government would take care that the emoluments thereof should not be spent abroad.[1] Such are the principal acts of Simon de Montfort, which most clearly justify his headship of the national-ecclesiastical party, foreshadow his church-policy, and together with his earlier career and tragic death for the liberties of England caused him to be styled the Second Martyr of Canterbury.[2]

Owing to the brief duration of his rule, much that Simon would have done he could not; the ultimate tendency of his policy must therefore be rather conjectured than known. It seems certain, however, that the author of the Mise of Lewes[3] and of the constitution[4] of 1264–1265 would have ruled England as

[1] Rymer, I., p. 444. June 25, 1264. Nec enim si secus egeritis, proventus archiepiscopales ad vos extra regnum de cetero deferri sustinebimus, set sicut onera recusatis ita et emolumenta vobis extra regnum agentibus, subtrahere curabimus in futuro.

[2] Wright, Pol. Songs, pp. 125–127. Mailros, pp. 211, 212. Non minus occubuit Simon pro justa ratione legitimarum possessionum Anglie, quam Thomas pro legitima ratione ecclesiarum Anglie olim occubuerat. The same chronicler devotes six pages, pp. 205–211, of his work to drawing an elaborate parallel between Simon Peter, the Rock of the Church, and Simon de Montfort, the Rock of the Church in the State.

[3] Rish., Chronicon, p. 37. Sel. Chart., p. 335, Mise of Lewes. Tertium: quod isti arbitri jurabunt quod eligant consiliarios indigenas tantum, quos ipsi regi et regno noverunt utiliores. Quartum: quod rex credat consiliariis suis sine personarum acceptione, in justitia exhibenda et in ministris officialibus vel ballivis suis de Anglicis tantummodo et indigenis creandis, constituendis. Stubbs' Const. Hist., II., p. 93, points out the intermediary position of the Mise of Lewes between the constitutions of 1258 and 1264–1265.

[4] Rymer, I., p. 443. Sel. Chart., p. 414. Extract from the De

a nation and with the aid of Englishmen. Of schemes of foreign conquest not a single trace exists. If one may be permitted to trust the analogy of a more modern time, Simon's apparent adoption of the first protective tariff[1] would have ushered in an era whose appropriate motto must have been "England for Englishmen."

The spirit of the great earl was chivalrous and noble; his statesmanship was of the highest order; but his patriotism or his ambition, or both, had placed him in an impossible position. Assuredly he was not of those who "fain would climb but that they fear to fall," and whither his towering ambition would have led him, no one can definitely say. From another standpoint, too, the permanence of his work was endangered. His impetuosity might easily have caused him, as it has so many others, to adopt political short cuts, and to

---

Ordinatione pro pace regni. Item ordinatum est quod predicti tres electores et consiliarii . . . et castrorum custodes et ceteri ballivi dom. regis, semper sint indigenæ. Ordained at London, in parliament, June, 1264. For the summons to the parliament of Jan. 20, 1265, *vide* Rymer, I., p. 449. Sel. Chart., p. 415.

[1] Wykes, p. 158. Walt. Hem., p. 306, includes the following among the Provisions of Oxford, but it possibly refers to this later occurrence. Statuerunt insuper quod lanæ terræ operarentur in Anglia nec alienigenis venderentur, et quod omnes uterentur pannis laneis infra limites terræ operatis, etc. The whole movement, however, seems not to have been original with de Montfort, but rather a reprisal for the legate's order: Omnes insuper, qui eis, in prædicta rebellione manentibus, arma, equos, bladum, vinum vel alia victualia ferrent in Angliam, vel ferri facerent ; . . . pari excommunicationis sententia innodavimus. Rymer, I., p. 447. Oct. 20, 1264. At the birth of the House of Commons, England set a precedent which America was glad to follow in the days of patriotic enthusiasm just before the Revolution.

impose upon the nation a constitution which was the result not of internal growth but of external will. The beneficence of the will would have made but little difference in the ultimate result. As it was, however, he lived just long enough to interpret the spirit of the nation and to justify its hopes, to set the broad seal to his own political greatness, and to educate a successor even greater than himself.[1] Grosseteste, Simon, and Edward are the links of the golden chain which bound England to national unity and completeness.

The jealousy and selfishness of the earl of Gloucester, rightly or wrongly based, had been the immediate cause of Leicester's death.[2] In the last subdivision of the reign, however, he somewhat retrieved his reputation.[3]

---

[1] Cf. Freeman, Hist. of the Norm. Conq., V., pp. 728, 729. Stubbs' Const. Hist., II., pp. 103, 104.

[2] For their quarrel, *vide* Rish., Chronicon, pp. 41, 42. Rish., Chronica, pp. 31, 32. Ant. Leg., p. 73. Osney, p. 162. Rymer, I., pp. 450, 455, 456. Dunst., p. 238. Trivet, p. 263. Walt. Hem., pp. 319, 320. Wykes, pp. 153, 160, 161. Wav., p. 358. Rob. Glouc., pp. 550, 551. Stubbs' Const. Hist., II., p. 98. Pauli, III., pp. 785, 786. Pauli, Sim. v. Mont., pp. 172, 173. Blaauw, pp. 224-232.

[3] (a) He restrained the king from his fury against the Disinherited. Rish., Chronicon, p. 59. Dunst., p. 245. (b) He favoured the Dictum of Kenilworth, and was one of the committee who drew it up. Sel. Chart., p. 419. Stat. of Realm, I., p. 12. Rish., Chronicon, p. 59. (c) He opposed the Marchers, the most radical of the royalists. Rish., Chronicon, pp. 59, 60. Rish., Chronica, pp. 45, 46. Dunst., p. 245. (d) He refused to march against Ely, revolted, and entered London, because he desired the removal of aliens and the reinstatement of the Disinherited. Rish., Chronicon, p. 60. Osney, pp. 199, 200. Dunst., p. 245. Trivet, p. 271. Cf. Rish., Chronica, p. 57. Ant. Leg., pp. 90-93. Wykes, pp. 198, 199. Winton., p. 105.

The intolerant madness[1] of the parliament of Winchester had disinherited the adherents of the earl of Leicester, and parted their lands and goods among the royalists; in Kenilworth, Axyholm, and Ely — that chosen home of English liberties, where Hereward fought the last battles of the Saxon and from whose neighbourhood at a later day came the most determined opponents of that monarch who sought to overthrow the system whose foundation Simon had just laid — rebellion still existed. It was hopeless from the start, for it possessed no unity of plan or action;[2] although the cry for the Provisions of Oxford still was stoutly raised,[3] the great desire of the insurgents was to win back their ancient patrimonies. They made a gallant fight, maintaining their position until men's minds had time to cool, and until a reaction against royal tyranny, the greed of the court, and the unheeding prodigality of the king, had once more set in. In a certain sense Earl Simon was still at their head: the

---

(e) His original compact with Edward at Ludlow, in 1264. Wykes, pp. 164, 165. (*f*) Final treaty with the king, June 16, 1267. Rymer, I., p. 472.

[1] *Vide* the royalist Wykes, p. 183. Post inopinatam Eveshamiæ triumphalem victoriam, rex et sui complices non sicut decuerat cautiores effecti, sed potius stultiores, etc. P. 219 (1268): Eodem anno rex sano fretus consilio promisit et statuit, quod exhæredati, quorum terras diversis personis minus consulte contulerat, etc. The actions speak for themselves. The date of the parliament was Sept. 8, 1265. Rymer, I., p. 462. Rish., Chronica, pp. 37, 38. Rish., Chronicon, pp. 48, 49. Osney, pp. 173, 178, 179. Ant. Leg., p. 76. Wykes, p. 176. Trivet, p. 267. Cf. Dunst., p. 239. Wav., p. 366.

[2] Cf. Osney, pp. 185, 186. Peterb., p. 18.

[3] Rish., Chronicon, pp. 60, 63, 64.

first sign of the coming reaction had been the popular canonization of the national hero,[1] and as the struggle approached its end, a special article in the Dictum of Kenilworth provided that henceforth no man should hail Leicester as a saint or mention his pretended miracles.[2] Harsh as the terms of this celebrated Dictum were, yet they were far milder than those of Winchester: the chief difficulty lay in the fact that they were not observed. What the strong hand of the Marchers had won, the Marchers sought to keep. At the critical moment the earl of Gloucester interposed. First he demanded that the covenant which Edward had made with him at Ludlow[3] should be kept; then, raising an army, he hastened to London. The city at first received him cautiously enough,[4] but later, exasperated

---

[1] A collection of Simon's alleged miracles is published in Halliwell's edition of Rish., Chronicon, under the title "Miracula Simonis de Montfort," pp. 67-110. For their immediate effect, *vide* Mail., p. 201. Rish., Chronicon, p. 49. Infra breve tempus suæ mortis, crebris cepit ostendere miraculis. Quid ergo? suspiria mutantur in laudis præconia, et revixit pristinæ lætitiæ magnitudo. In this movement the Minorites played an interesting part. Mail., p. 212. Post occubitum vero Simonis in mortem pretiosam, fratres Minores, quos ipse dilexerat religioso more, qui et ipsi conscii fuerunt conscientie ejus in plurimis, materiam loquendi sumentes de vita ejus, ex optimis gestis ejus venerandam de illo ediderunt hystoriam, sc. lectiones, responsoria, versus, hymnum et alia que pertinent ad decus unius martirie et honorem.

[2] Sel. Chart., pp. 420, 421. Stat. Realm, I., p. 13.

[3] Wykes, pp. 164, 165. (1) To preserve the ancient laws, good and approved. (2) To abolish evil customs. (3) To urge the king to remove aliens from the realm and council. (4) Not to allow aliens to be castle-guards or administrators. (5) Et quod res indigenarum sibi fidelium consilio regeretur.

[4] Ant. Leg., p. 90.

by the heavy penalties [1] which the king, incapable alike of learning by experience and of self-restraint, had inflicted upon them, de Montfort's following gave him their unqualified support.[2] Many of the Ely rebels speedily joined him,[3] and the royal army dared not storm the city. For the last time in the Barons' War, Richard of Germany appeared in his oft-repeated rôle of mediator, and this time with success.[4] Gloucester's rising had ensured the relief of the Disinherited; their protracted resistance had given a second object-lesson to the wielders of the royal power, had secured for themselves through the Dictum of Kenilworth the ultimate enjoyment of their ancestral estates, and had stopped the king and the radical party in their headlong career of spoliation. Their revolt had therefore tended to the formation of a more lasting and beneficent peace.

All parties, in truth, were heartily weary of the war,

---

[1] For Henry's injudicious treatment of London in suspending the city charter, imprisoning citizens in violation of his safe conduct, confiscating their goods, and levying a heavy fine (20,000 marks) for the repurchase of peace, *vide* Nangis, I., p. 229. Rish., Chronica, p. 38. Fabyan, pp. 360-364. Winton., p. 103. Ant. Leg., pp. 77-80. Trivet, p. 267. Rob. Glouc., p. 561. Wav., p. 366, 367. Shirley, II., pp. 293, 294. Rymer, I., p. 464. Wykes, pp. 177, 178, 184, 176. Ibique (Wyndeshoriam) venientes cives Londoniarum sub specie treviarum, majores eorum minus honeste quam regiam decebat dignitatem de procerum suorum concilio captivavit et captivatos carcerali custodiæ mancipavit, etc.

[2] Ant. Leg., p. 91. Minutus populus.

[3] Wykes, p. 199. Winton., p. 105. Dunst., p. 245. Ant. Leg., p. 90.

[4] Rymer, I., p. 472. Rish., Chronica, p. 57. Osney, p. 205. Ant. Leg., p. 92. Dunst., p. 246. Wykes, p. 205. Trivet, p. 272.

when on the 18th of November, 1267, the Statute of Marlborough[1] brought it to a close. Ely had already surrendered to Prince Edward, peace had been made with Llewellyn, the barons' stanch ally,[2] the fields had yielded up abundant harvests,[3] and kindly legislation was the one thing needed to heal the wounds of war. Never, therefore, was legal enactment more timely than this notable Statute of Marlborough. "It was Provided" — so runs the preamble[4] — "and established and ordained (that) (whereas the Realm of England having been of late depressed by manifold Troubles and the evils of Dissensions, standeth in need of a Reform of the Laws and Usages, whereby the Peace and Tranquillity of the People may be preserved, whereto it behoved the King and his liege men to apply an wholesome Remedy) the Provisions, Ordinances, and Statutes underwritten should be firmly and inviolably observed by all the People of the same Realm, as well high as low, forever." No less admirable than the promise of its preamble was the statute's general spirit. The desire to make the penalty correspond to the offence was throughout predominant, and the incorporation of the reforms[5] established by the baronial government of 1259 at the instance of the knights was a pledge of

---

[1] Mentioned by Trivet, p. 274. Cont. Mat. Par., p. 1006. Stat. of Realm, I., pp. 19–25.

[2] Sept. 29, 1267. Rymer, I., pp. 473, 474.

[3] Wykes, p. 211.

[4] Stat. of Realm, I., p. 19, n. 1.

[5] Provisions of Westminster. Burt., p. 480 *et seq.* Sel. Chart., pp. 401–405. Stat. of Realm, I., pp. 8–11.

lasting amity. The great Charters of Liberty were solemnly confirmed,[1] and the presence of the legate guaranteed immunity from Rome.

The following year the clergy granted a tenth for the relief of the Disinherited,[2] and at the January parliament of London in 1271, their lands were finally restored.[3] By an ordinance of the 12th of February, 1270, a permanent reform of the treasury, that earlier seat of unlimited prodigality and wrong, had already been effected.[4] More than all, the course of nature had been busily at work, and the aliens around whom the abuses of the reign had centred had dropped off one by one. Henry, too, was growing old, and his energies for good and ill were slackening. Through the administration of the state by a prince whose aims and sympathies were deeply national, and whose councillors were to be selected from that younger generation whose hearts were once as wax[5] in the moulding hands of Simon de Montfort, England was passing to happier days, — days of national unity and constitutional completeness.

---

[1] Art. V. "The Great Charter shall be observed in all his articles, as well in such as pertain to the king, as to other. . . ."

[2] Wykes, pp. 219, 220. Peterb., p. 19. "Quadragesima."

[3] Sel. Chart., p. 337. Winton., p. 110. Per communem assensum dom. Ricardi, regis Alemanniæ, Gilberti com. Gloverniæ, Philippi Basset et aliorum.

[4] Rymer, I., p. 483. Ordinationes super statu scaccarii Regis.

[5] Wykes, pp. 133, 134. Cum junioribus Angliæ pueris . . . quos vere et autonomatice pueros nominare possumus, qui tanquam cera liquescens ductiles ad quamlibet formam, etc.

PART III

PARTIES AND PRINCIPLES

THROUGH the infinite variety of external events which makes the political history of the reign of Henry III. so difficult of comprehension, the influence of two parties — royalist and national — can always be discerned with more or less clearness. The personnel of the parties changes from time to time, and the political devices which are employed to curb the royal power also vary constantly, yet underneath the surface the motive-power remains ever the same and urges the state unceasingly along the road of constitutional progress.

In the early part of Henry's reign — while Peter des Roches was active — the royalist party consisted mainly of the favourers of aliens and the favourers of Rome. These two classes were practically identical, and throughout nearly the whole of Henry's independent reign formed the basis of his power. Their policy was selfish, unconstitutional, and unnational. In the later years of the Barons' War this party was joined by the Marchers, and in their company became identified with the policy of reaction and spoliation which triumphed at Winchester. As soon, however, as it was known at Rome that by the victory of Evesham the royal power had been re-established, the pope reverted to the traditional papal policy of clemency at the moment of success, and counselled moderation.[1] At this time the Roman branch of the royalist party abandoned the Marchers and acted in unison with a second section of the king's supporters which belonged to the English baronage. At various periods before the Mad Parliament, individual nobles had sided with the king,[2] but usually from more or less temporary reasons of personal advantage. Since the dissolution of that body, and particularly since the outbreak of the civil war, these fugitive elements had become permanently attached to the crown and formed the nucleus of the second section of the royal party. Many of its members had been influenced by jealousy or self-seeking to desert the nationalists,[3] but many others were doubtless convinced that baronial rule meant anarchy, and that through the subversion of the monarchy the existence of the state was threatened. Among the latter class were numbered Richard of Germany, his son

---

[1] Rymer, I., p. 463. Oct. 4, 1265. Celsitudinem regiam monemus, etc., sano tibi consilio in remissionem nichilominus peccaminum suadentes, quatinus diligenter attendens, quod clementia firmat imperium . . . te clementem exhibeas, et benignitate utaris ; . . . Plures etenim ad tuum, et ipsius, aliorumque tuorum amorem humanitas remissionis alliciet, quam poenæ duritia castigaret ; cum fervor vindictæ paucorum odium reprimat, multorum irritet.

[2] As in 1255. At the Mad Parliament itself the king was not without supporters, but his "party was very poor in the historic names of England." Stubbs' Const. Hist., II., p. 78.

[3] Rish., Chronicon, pp. 17, 18. Rish., Chronica, pp. 12, 13. Trivet, p. 253.

Henry, Gilbert of Gloucester, the Earl Marshall, Philip Basset, and Edward himself.[1] It is needless to say that their programme was national in character, and was based on the observance of the Charters. With the assistance of the legate they withstood the violence of the Marchers,[2] drew up and enforced the Dictum of Kenilworth, and in the Statute of Marlborough conceded nearly all which had been enacted by the Mad Parliament at Oxford.[3] The national party[4] had been defeated in war, but its spirit was still abroad in the land, and the noblest part of its work was destined to be preserved.

---

[1] Cf. Rish., Chronicon, p. 65. Also *supra*, p. 199, n. 3.

[2] Rish., Chronicon, pp. 57, 59, 65. Chronica, pp. 45, 46.

[3] Cf. B. Cotton, p. 143 (1267). Evidently referring to the Statute of Marlborough, he writes: "Eodem anno rex concessit statuta Oxoniæ observari, exceptis paucis." The appointment of the great officers and sheriffs was left in the king's hands. Cf. Stubbs' Const. Hist., II., p. 101.

[4] The movement of parties from 1258–1267 had been very peculiar. Broadly speaking, in October, 1258, the royal party, in so far as it still existed, was entirely unnational; the party of reform entirely national. One wing of the latter party was national and aristocratic; another was national and democratic in tendency, the wing which we have called the national-ecclesiastical. It was the gradual falling away of the first wing to the king's side which produced a royalist-national party. The ultimate completion of the national programme and of the national constitution was due solely to the persistence of the national-democratic wing, which is therefore the national party par excellence. That part of its work which was embodied in the Statute of Marlborough was preserved mainly by the influence of the royalist-national party, headed by the leaders above mentioned, assisted by the legate, and *impelled by the occurrences since the parliament of Winchester*. It was reserved for Edward to preserve, quicken, and complete the constitutional development.

During the struggle the king had sought in all quarters to obtain allies. At Lewes the great Scotch lords had fought beneath his banner.[1] By personal visits to France he had sought to counteract the influence of Simon de Montfort, and had at last succeeded in winning Louis to his side through the natural influence of autocratic ideas, the support of Rome, and the kinship of the queens [2] of France and England. But throughout all, Henry's steadiest ally was Rome.

Immediately after the promulgation of the Provisions of Oxford, the pope had entered upon a policy of evasion toward the barons and of invitation toward the king; the papal bulls of dispensation proclaimed the result. Henceforth the spiritual weapons of the papacy were unreservedly at his command. The Award of Amiens was hastily confirmed, and all recalcitrants were visited with spiritual penalties.[3] After the battle of Lewes, Guy Foulquois, cardinal-bishop of Sabina, was sent at the request of the queen and the aliens as legate of the Apostolic See to England,[4] but the barons wisely forbade [5] him to enter. He was therefore forced to content himself with summoning the foremost pre-

---

[1] Dunst., p. 232. Rish., Chronicon, pp. 26, 33. Mail., p. 192. Trivet, p. 260.

[2] Cf. Dunst., p. 227. Rex vero Franciæ ad instantiam uxoris suæ et reginæ Angliæ, ut dictum est, etc. (1264).

[3] Rymer, I., pp. 436–438.

[4] Rish., Chronicon, p. 38. Dunst., p. 233. Osney, p. 151.

[5] Rish., Chronicon, p. 30. Dunst., p. 241. Wykes, p. 155. Rymer, I., p. 447. Naugis, I., p. 225. Cf. Rish., Chronica, page 31.

lates of the national party to Boulogne,¹ and ordering them to publish his decree in England.² Leicester, Gloucester, and Roger of Norfolk were excommunicated by name, and all their adherents *en masse;* London and the Cinq Ports were placed by name under interdict, and all other places and lands adhering or belonging to the barons shared the same fate under a general sentence. The importation of arms, food, and wine was forbidden, and the Provisions of Oxford, and all legislation dependent upon them, were declared null and void.³ The cardinal had been sent ostensibly as an angel of peace, but he brought not peace but a sword.⁴ Had Rome had its will, de Montfort's parliament had never seen the light.

The bulls of excommunication had been entrusted to the bishops to be carried into England, but when the bold mariners of the Cinq Ports sailed out and seized the documents, they met with no resistance.⁵ The

---

[1] London, Worcester, Chichester, Winchester, *et al.* Wykes, p. 156. Qui comitis et baronum præcipue fautores extiterant. Dunst., p. 234. Trivet, p. 268. Cf. Rish., Chronicon, p. 39, and Rymer, I., pp. 446, 447.

[2] Rish., Chronicon, pp. 38, 39. Wykes, p. 156.

[3] Rymer, I., pp. 447, 448. Nov. 20, 1264. Cf. Rymer, I., p. 459. Ad futuram rei memoriam, Sept. 13, 1265.

[4] Rish., Chronicon, p. 38. Wykes, p. 155. Cf. Dunst., p. 233. Habens potestatem utriusque gladii: et per unum, (ut) episcopos, barones Angliæ excommunicare nolentes, deponeret; et per alium, quosdam barones usque ad triginta exhæredaret.

[5] Wykes, pp. 156, 157. Obtento quidem super hoc rescripto apostolico, pelago se credentes (episcopi), sponte nescio vel invite, comprehensi sunt in mari a Quinque Portuensibus, qui scripta eorum autentica dilaniata minuatim vel concisa projecerunt in mare, etc.

great canon of William the Conqueror had been long obsolete, but in the presence of a mighty national sentiment it was needed no longer. At a great meeting of the clergy a unanimous appeal against the legate's action was taken; it was approved later by the barons, and sent under their seal to Rome.[1] Shortly afterwards the legate himself became pope Clement IV. No peace with Rome was possible. About the first of November, 1265, Cardinal Ottobon reached England.[2] The battle had then been fought and won, and he could at once enter upon the congenial task of punishing those prelates who, in defence of their country's liberties, had braved the thunders of Rome. The noble Walter of Worcester was soon beyond his reach, "snatched that he might not see evil days,"[3] but the bishops of Chichester, Winchester, and London were sent to Rome to await the pleasure of the pope.[4] Ottobon also diverted to the uses of the king and Edward the tenth which had been granted to de Montfort by the prelates to guard England against invasion,[5] and later procured for the king the grant of a tenth for three years.[6] This conduct, together with the

---

[1] Rish., Chronicon, p. 39. Dunst., p. 234.
[2] Dunst., p. 240. Wav., p. 367.   [3] Wykes, p. 180.
[4] Wykes, pp. 185-187. Ant. Leg., p. 83. Osney, pp. 180-182. Dunst., pp. 240, 241. Cf. Rymer, I., p. 463. Wykes gives the fullest account. Winchester died. Lincoln was finally received to favour. "Hen. de Sandwyz, episc. Lond. qui propter familiaritatem Simonis de M. . . . in curia dom. Papæ perduravit." Dunst., p. 247.
[5] Rymer, I., pp. 458, 462 (1265).
[6] £60,000 Tours of this latter sum were used to pay the debts which the queen had contracted in France in behalf of her hus-

honours[1] paid him by the king, made it appear exceedingly doubtful whether his presence would conduce ultimately to harmony or not. In other respects, however, he used his power wisely; at Axyholm,[2] Kenilworth,[3] and Ely[4] he favoured arbitration, employing excommunication simply as a means to that end; the Dictum of Kenilworth[5] and the final peace with Llewellyn[6] were largely due to his influence, and he twice confirmed the royal charters.[7] In many respects his behaviour resembles Gualo's, and in general the parallel between the papal policy at this crisis and in the reign of John is remarkably close. At neither time did it favour English liberty, except in so far as was necessary to secure its own future success.

In their search for allies the barons, as well as the king, had entered France; although they ultimately lost Louis' support, they had succeeded, nevertheless, through the personal ascendency of Leicester,[8] in re-

---

band during his captivity. Rymer, I., p. 473. Rish., Chronicon, pp. 60, 61. Rish., Chronica, p. 47. Wykes, p. 213. Cf. Dunst., p. 244.

[1] Rish., Chronicon, p. 59. At Christmas. Legato in sedili regio collocato, singulisque ferculis coram eo primitus appositis, et postremo coram rege, etc.

[2] Rish., Chronicon, p. 50. Wav., p. 368.

[3] Rish., Chronicon, pp. 54, 55. Wykes, p. 191. Wav., p. 371.

[4] Rish., Chronicon, p. 62. Dunst., p. 241. Wykes, p. 196.

[5] Osney, p. 191. Rish., Chronicon, pp. 57-59. Ant. Leg., p. 88. Winton., p. 104. Wav., p. 372. Dunst., p. 242.

[6] Rymer, I., pp. 467, 473, 474. Trivet, p. 272. Rish., Chronica, p. 58. Winton., p. 105.

[7] Ant. Leg., p. 89. Cf. Ant. Leg., pp. 87, 88, and Wav., p. 371.

[8] For the universal respect which was entertained for Leicester in

taining the friendship of many influential men. The chief advantage, however, which this fact afforded seems to have been the facilitation of many arbitrations of doubtful utility.

The assistance of the Welsh was of vastly more importance to the national party — especially after hostilities became inevitable. No painful negotiations were ever needed to secure the support of these natural allies. At the Hokeday parliament of 1258 Leicester and Gloucester had blushed at de Valence's charge of complicity — although, probably, their complicity at this time was limited to a secret feeling of joy at unexpected assistance. When the baronage and king were at variance, Llewellyn was apt to break out of bounds; when peace existed between them, he felt that discretion was valour's better part.[1] It was not until the closing days of the Barons' War that Llewellyn was formally leagued[2] with de Montfort, but an informal understanding evidently subsisted between them at a much earlier date. Had de Montfort remained at the helm of state, Wales certainly would not have been incorporated with England in the year 1284.

Throughout Henry's reign, the barons had had the welfare of England more or less at heart. In the earlier periods, while Langton was primate and an

---

France, *vide ex grege*, the offer of the regency (Mat. Par. V., pp. 371, 372, 415), and the French estimate of de Valence's speech to Leicester in the Hokeday parliament (Mat. Par., V., p. 703). Perhaps it was on account of the Sicilian affair that Anjou was his friend. Mat. West., p. 385.

[1] Mat. Par., V., p. 727.   [2] Rymer, I., p. 457. June 22, 1265.

earl of Pembroke or a Hubert de Burgh headed an undivided baronage, they had actually wrought great good. Later came an era of confusion. No permanent union existed between the barons and the national party in the church; the king was in the hands of aliens; the church was plundered by both king and pope; the baronage had no acknowledged head, and constant jealousies and bitter rivalries except at rare intervals divided their ranks and destroyed their power. It was not until the multiform aggressions of the king upon both state and church had become utterly unbearable that the barons definitely and finally took their stand upon the technicalities [1] of Magna Charta as the basis for resistance; and it was not until the behaviour of Rustand had roused the prelates and the clergy to a pitch of desperation that the national wing of the church yielded to the solicitations of the baronage and formed with them a permanent union.[2] At the opening of the Mad Parliament the national party was apparently a unit. All the elements which are indispensable for a great revolution were then present in England. Magnificent aspirations for political freedom and national rights were accompanied by distinct grievances which pressed heavily upon the members of all classes, from the greatest of the barons to the least of the "populi minuti" of the cities. There were plenty of leaders to voice the general discontent, whether at the corners of the city streets, in the remote country-

---

[1] Mat. Par., V., p. 520 (1255).
[2] *Ibid.*, V., pp. 525, 553 (1256).

villages and manors, in the convocation of the clergy, or the halls of parliament. There was no dearth of the military talent necessary to ensure success, and zeal for religion and the freedom of the church was at the very heart of the movement and promised the crown of martyrdom to all who fell in the strife. Unfortunately, but inevitably, there were also present, especially among the leaders, all the lower motives of selfish gain and personal aggrandizement and petty jealousies. It is true that a considerable period elapsed before these made their appearance in the light of day, but, in reality, almost from the first the baronage was divided by fundamental differences into two camps:[1] when these differences became apparent, the lower motives accentuated them and led to hopeless disunion.

The keynote of the constitutional and military conflicts of the reign of Henry III. is the aspiration for separate national existence and for a government national in both form and spirit and in the personnel of the administration. Without this aspiration the Barons' War could no more have come to pass than the First Crusade could have occurred without the fundamental inspiration of religion. From the contest against foreign elements the whole reign gets its colour, literature, and politics alike.

Among prose writers, Matthew Paris, the first great national historian, makes his appearance, and around him is clustered a whole galaxy of lesser lights. Of

---

[1] *Vide infra*, pp. 218, 219.

all contemporary English historiographers Thomas Wykes alone is deeply royalist in sympathies, — yet even he seems forced to take Prince Edward for his hero and excuse the king. In the poetical literature the same tendency is still more deeply marked. With scarcely an exception the poems which are extant deal with political subjects, and without a single exception these favour the national side. In connection with the Barons' War the first political poem in English makes its appearance, for the first time the English language is used[1] in public documents, and knowledge of the English tongue is made in certain sections of the country the test of patriotism.

The central political issues of the reign are also deeply national: first, the protection of the church from the ravages of a denationalizing king and an alien head; second, the maintenance of the inviolability of the Great Charter — the pledge of national freedom and the concrete expression of the spirit of the laws; and third, the administration of the government by men of English birth and education. The second issue involved all political interests of permanent value; a successful struggle for the third was the necessary prelude to the attainment of the second; and the association of the religious question with them both, lent to the revolt of the barons the aspect of a holy war.[2] The maintenance of the Charter with all which it involved was the most important issue, as being in itself

---

[1] In 1258. [2] Cf. *infra*, pp. 223, 224.

the supreme end; the third issue, however, was the only direct means to that end and, as such, was closest to the heart of every patriot.

It was upon this point, too, that the national pride had been most aggrieved. The alienation of London from the crown, the king's ill-treatment of Simon de Montfort, his general misgovernment and prodigality, his costly foreign wars and even the trebly foolish acceptance of the Sicilian crown, pale into insignificance as a cause of revolution compared with his denationalization of the English church and state through the introduction of aliens. Was not this the root of the evil? They supplanted the native English in the affections of their prince, usurped their places at the council-board and in the church, outraged the personal dignity of the English barons by their pride and arrogance, invaded the rights of the people, fostered the king's unnational visions of greatness abroad, formed the nucleus of almost every governmental abuse in the treasury and the department of justice, sought to warp the English constitution from its natural Anglo-Saxon tendencies and to substitute mere absolutism, and finally, through their mastery of the royal castles, threatened to make their power permanent. Intermarriage with these aliens, though the king's own relatives in part, was held to contaminate the ancient English blood.[1]

All patriots were therefore determined that England

---

[1] Mat. Par., V., p. 363. Also the Petitions at Oxford. *Vide supra*, pp. 75, 76, and n. 2, and p. 167.

should be ruled by Englishmen. Upon this plea Simon de Montfort himself was once driven from the seat of council and from the land by less worthy men than he; and after he had won the highest place in the gift of the nation, specious treachery renewed this charge to justify itself. It was largely this question which gave the decisive turn to the constitutional struggles of the reign and determined their outward form. Because Henry drove the great officers from power and substituted for them at the treasury, chancery, and council-chamber commissions of men of lesser note and often of alien extraction, the barons were directly forced to demand the right of nominating the three great officers of state.[1] This demand was based, according to baronial theory, upon the Magna Charta, was accompanied by the determination to purify the royal council by the exclusion of aliens, and ultimately expanded, under stress of circumstances, to a demand for the appointment of a permanent executive committee. This practical programme placed the Magna Charta in the forefront of the battle; the regency which existed during the king's minority had furnished abundant precedents for its unconscious expansion,[2] and the result was the Provisions of Oxford.

This question of the governance of England by Eng-

---

[1] *Vide supra*, pp. 69, 70. Cf. Gneist, Eng. Ver. Gesch., p. 269. Diese büreaukratische Gestalt eben gab jeder Einwirkung der Magnaten sofort die Richtung auf Besetzung der Grossämter und des Sheriffamts. He does not mention aliens in this connection, however.

[2] Cf. Stubbs' Const. Hist., II., pp. 40, 41.

lishmen kept increasing in importance as the denationalization of the state progressed, and finally, as the practical embodiment of all other questions and as the sole means to the supreme end, overshadowed all other issues and made the conflict no less directly national in outward form than in its spirit. The truth of this statement is best attested by certain documents drawn up at the most critical periods of the combat. First, the Petition of the Barons at Oxford demanded, among other things, the delivery of the royal castles into English hands. Second, in accordance with this Petition it was legally enacted at the Oxford parliament that the castles should be restored at once, and that all opponents of the Provisions of Oxford should be considered public enemies. This was followed immediately by the expulsion of the Poitevins and all other aliens who refused to take the oath. Shortly afterwards, significantly enough, the divisions in the ranks of the baronage begin. Third, about the 24th of June, 1263, the barons offered to submit the Provisions of Oxford to arbitrators who should correct, explain, or expunge whatever was prejudicial to the royal power and the welfare of the realm, but insisted on the administration of the state by men of English birth.[1] Fourth, this same condition was inserted in the peace which was actually made by the king and barons in London in July of the same year.[2] Fifth — and most conclusively

---

[1] Ant. Leg., p. 54. Cited *supra*, p. 189, n. 2.
[2] Trivet, p. 252. Ant. Leg., pp. 55, 56. Rish., Chronicon, p. 13. Et quod regno de cætero per indigenas et naturales terræ et utiles sub. dom. rege gubernetur.

— after Louis had made his formal Award at Amiens and when civil war seemed unavoidable, the barons announced to the king that they would assent to the Dictum, provided that he would annul the article which allowed the employment of aliens and provided that he would remove them from the realm and administer the state through English agents.[1] This proviso was refused, and therefore became the *sole cause*, *officially recognized*, of the war of 1264. Sixth, the same condition forms the basis of the Mise of Lewes and is excepted from French arbitration.[2] Finally, it was enacted in the constitution of 1264-1265, that all members of the executive councils, all custodians of castles, and all bailiffs of the king should be indigenous.

On all the points which have been mentioned, the two wings of the baronage were at first perfectly agreed. The surrender of the castles, the expulsion of refractory aliens, the appointment by the baronage of the three great officers of state, the reform of certain abuses in the administration of the treasury, chancery, and department of justice, the confirmation of the Charters, the rescue of the church from spoliation, and the establishment of a permanent council of nobles with legislative and executive power — these seemed essential to all. Experience justified the first five points, and in the end they were practically won. As to the sixth, however desirable in point of fact the rescue of the

---

[1] *Supra*, p. 193, n. 1. Quod alienigenis ab Anglia remotis per indigenas gubernetur.
[2] Rish., Chronicon, p. 37. Sel. Chart., p. 335.

church might seem to all, yet the members of the conservative wing of the party doubtless were thinking more of their lost rights of patronage and their added burdens of national taxation than of spiritual things, while it was not yet revealed to statesmanship that, through the essential weakness of the church as a privileged and isolated body possessed of vast wealth but destitute of secular means of defence, the day would come when rescue from the pope of Rome meant simply slavery to the king of England.[1] The insurrection of the barons produced temporary relief for the church, but no permanent benefits.

The last point — the executive council — was wholly new in fact, though not in theory. "Under John, the barons had sought to organize and legalize rebellion in advance; under Henry III. they endeavoured to organize not rebellion, but power, and to win guarantees not for war, but for the very constitution of the government. Unable to limit duly the authority of the king, they sought to appropriate it for themselves — in a word, to substitute for the monarchy an oligarchy."[2] It was in connection with this oligarchy — that is, in connection with the relation of the executive council of fifteen to the basis of the state — that the fundamental differences between the two sections of the baronage were finally displayed.

The first of these two sections was the old baronial

---

[1] B. Cotton, p. 322. Unde clericalis ordo vilissimus et vilior plebe reputabatur. 1296.

[2] Guizot, Histoire des Origines, etc., II., pp. 164, 165.

party; its leader was the earl of Gloucester, and its ultimate tendencies were conservative and aristocratic. The second was the national-ecclesiastical party; it had been founded by Grosseteste, was led by Simon de Montfort in close association with Walter of Worcester and Stephen of Chichester, and contained within its membership all, or nearly all, the constructive talent of the day. Its ultimate tendencies were popular and progressive. The final political objects and points of view of these two parties were as far apart as the poles. The problem of the times, as it presented itself in 1258, and afterwards, to the mind of Richard of Gloucester and his party, was essentially as follows: In what way shall the power of the monarch be so limited as to put an end to the evils of alien influence in state and church, and to secure the predominance of the native English baronage in the councils of the nation?[1] Their statement of the problem was selfish and faulty, and its solution was therefore incorrect. The terms were too limited in application, and the agency for the correction of abuses rested upon too narrow a basis.

De Montfort's presentation of the question would have been much broader: In what way shall the power of the crown be so limited as to put an end to the evils of alien influence in church and state and to secure the full rights of all the English nation?

The problem, however, was far larger than it at first appeared, and the key to its full solution could not,

---

[1] Cf. Stubbs' Const. Hist., II., p. 83.   Rish., Chronicon, p. 19.

in the very nature of things, be consciously in the possession of any man of the time. It was essentially a problem of a much more recent period. The growth of the nation postulated the growth of the constitution. The struggle for the Charter had already developed into a struggle for the principles which it implicitly contained, and the great council of the barons was already inadequate to give expression to the wishes of the nation. The twelfth century had developed the Anglo-Saxon organs of local self-government, and endowed the principal towns with charters, — bringing both into close connection with the central government. The work of the thirteenth century was to complete this development by extending the Anglo-Saxon principle of representation in the shire court to the great council of the nation,[1] giving to the higher classes of the commonalty a voice in all matters pertaining to the common weal. Herein lies the culmination of the national movement and the great significance of the Barons' War. On one side it was a protest against papal usurpations and the misuse of royal power; on the other, by compelling de Montfort's party to rely upon the support of the people against the crown, it hastened an almost inevitable constitutional development by broadening the basis of the central government. The smaller struggle, as we can see to-day, was inextricably involved in the greater — a fact which would alone account for the failure of the Provisions

---

[1] Gardiner and Mullinger's Eng. Hist. for Students, p. 62.

of Oxford to fetter the king and accomplish permanent reform. When to this the mutual jealousies of the barons, the diversity of their aims, and the friction necessarily involved in daily administration are added, it causes no wonder to learn that the Oxford plan of government completely failed.

The evidence for the political doctrines at the base of the national movement at the moment of its culmination between the battles of Lewes and Evesham, rests partly upon theoretical, partly on practical grounds. Of the latter, the parliament [1] which met at London on the 20th of January, 1265, is the most memorable and significant. Of the former, the poem [2] entitled the *Battle of Lewes* is scarcely less striking.

This poem is the confession of the political faith of the party of Simon de Montfort. As Freeman has so eloquently said,[3] the word "baron" in connection with this war seems to have reverted to its original signification. As the sword was once glorified by Halfred the Scald, so throughout this whole poem ring the words "communitas" and "universitas."

> "I miss the bright word in one
> Of thy measures and thy rhymes."
> And Halfred the Scald replied,
> "In another 'twas multiplied
> Three times."

There are no more complaints of the prevalence of irre-

---

[1] Writ, Rymer, I., p. 449. Sel. Chart., p. 415.
[2] Wright's Pol. Songs, pp. 72 *et seq.*
[3] Freeman, Norm. Conq., V., p. 728.

ligion, as in the songs of former days; the victory of Earl Simon has brought new life to England.

> Jam respirat Anglia, sperans libertatem,
> Cui Dei gratia det prosperitatem.[1]

In a vein worthy of Charles Sumner at his best, the author proceeds to magnify the claims of the Higher Law.

An analysis of the poem reveals its division into five parts.[2]

Victory, the salvation of England, due to God alone, is the theme of the prelude. The party of the king deservedly succumbed, for it was perjured, excommunicate, and guilty on numerous occasions of violence against the holy church.[3]

Part II. invokes upon Simon the blessing of God in recompense for his liberation of the English people,[4] and defends[5] him against malicious charges of treason and sedition by asserting his faithfulness to the point of death, by reciting the all but miraculous circumstances of his victory at Lewes, — the battle of a true Gideon,[6] — by ascribing the overthrow of the royalists

---

[1] Lines 9, 10.

[2] I., lines 1–64; II., 65–416; III., 417–484; IV., 485–846; V., 847 to the end. The poem is about as long as the sixth book of the Æneid.

[3] Part I., lines 1–64.

[4] Lines 65, 66:

> Benedicat dominus S. de Monte-Forti!
> Suis nichilominus natis et cohorti.

Lines 79–184.

[6] Elsewhere, line 149, Simon is a David —

> Golias prosternitur projecta lapilli.

immediately to their pride, cruelty, and filthy debauchery before the combat,[1] and by retorting the charge of unknightly and dishonourable conduct upon Simon's adversaries.[2] With the exception of a short digression[3] upon the evils attending the presence of aliens in England, and upon the baleful character of their policy,[4] the remainder[5] of the second section of the poem is devoted to the Glorification of Simon de Montfort. His equity,[6] steadfastness in reforming the state, and utter faithfulness to his oath to maintain the Provisions of Oxford, might well be imitated by others. His general importance to England could not be overrated; in him the stone which the builders rejected had indeed become the head of the corner;[7] to him alone the peaceful unity of England was ascribed.

> Fides et fidelitas Symonis solius
> Fit pacis integritas Angliæ totius.[8]

He was the rescuer of the oppressed and the chastiser of the proud,[9] fighting a fight enjoined by necessity and duty. He was the shield of England and its defence against the assaults of the aliens; no time server was

---

[1] Cf. Blaauw, p. 145. [2] Lines 167-170. [3] Lines 281-316.
[4] Lines 281-284 :
> Nam quidam studuerant Anglorum delere
> Nomen, quos jam cæperant exosos habere,
> Contra quos opposuit Deus medicinam,
> Ipsorum cum noluit subitam ruinam.

[5] Lines 185-416. [6] Line 185.
[7] Lines 261, 262. [8] Lines 267, 268.
[9] Lines 269-281.

he, but the type of pure altruism.[1] In fine, Simon was God's earthly champion, and his enemies were therefore hostile to England, the church, and to God. With a devout ascription of all the glory to the Deity and with the expression of an infinite yearning that he may perfect his good work, the second section of the poem closes.[2]

Part III.[3] delineates the character of Edward. His cognizance is the leopard, and it is remarkably appropriate. He is indeed a lion for bravery, pride, and ferocity, a pard for inconstancy and fickleness. An earnest exhortation for a change of conduct follows, coupled with a warning. Even the king is not above the laws;[4] no man can rule who will not keep the laws,[5] nor should the electors[6] choose such a one for king. Therefore,

> Si regnum desideras, leges venerare.[7]

The fourth[8] part of the poem discusses the respective attitudes of the existent parties toward the constitution, and the true relations of any king, council, and people.

---

[1] Lines 345, 346:

> Non sic venerabilis S. de Monte-Forti,
> Qui se Christo similis dat pro multis morti.

[2] Lines 400–414.   [3] Lines 417–484.

[4] Lines 445, 446:

> Nam rex omnis regitur legibus quas legit;
> Rex Saül repellitur, quia leges fregit.

[5] Line 450:

> Quod non potest regere qui non servat legem.

[6] Ad quos spectat.   [7] Line 455.   [8] Lines 485–846.

The first topic is mainly practical; it treats of the king's plea,[1] the barons' plea,[2] and the refutation[3] of the king's plea by the author.

The royalist position is as follows. A king desires to be free and ought to be so; but unless he can do whatever he pleases, he is unfree, therefore no king.[4] The magnates exceed their office, for they rightfully have no voice in the appointment of sheriffs,[5] constables, or the three great officers of state. All appointments should be made at the king's discretion and he should be free to select his advisers from all men and from all lands. His will should have the force of law. — Each earl in his earldom is at liberty to exercise these rights, and should a prince be less free than his vassal?[6] The magnates are encroaching on the king's prerogative; by means of sedition they seek to enslave him, destroy his princely dignity, and disinherit him, so that he may not exercise the full untrammelled power of his predecessors.

The baronial position is as follows. They desire, not to injure the royal honour, but to reform and magnify the princely office. This they have the right to do, for as it is their duty to defend the kingdom and the honour of the king whenever the realm is attacked in open warfare or endangered by invasion, so also is it

---

[1] Lines 485–526. [2] Lines 527–626.
[3] Lines 627–700. [4] Lines 489–492.
[5] Lines 493, 494, "quos præferret Suis comitatibus" is erroneously rendered by Wright, "prefer to his earldoms."
[6] This argument had been used in the parliament of 1248. Cf. Mat. Par., V., p. 20.

their duty to protect them both from the more insidious attacks of evil counsellors and aliens. These are real enemies of king and realm, for they seek by flattery to advance themselves, and by lying, to trample on the natives. They subvert the constitution, impoverish the commonalty[1] for their own ostentation, pervert and defeat the ends of justice, humiliate the rightful rulers of the land, and are in no respect less injurious than an open foreign enemy. Therefore, whether the king innocently, but misguidedly, assents to measures which are prejudicial to the welfare of the realm, or whether he acts with malice prepense in order to set his own power above the laws, the baronage in either case has an undoubted right to interfere. Further, since they are the necessary instruments for securing the safety of the state against assaults from without and within, it is likewise both their duty and their right to introduce reforms which not only tend to purify and regenerate the realm, but which also, by lessening the grievous rigour of the laws, are pleasing in the sight of God.[2] "For the oppression of the people pleaseth not God, but rather is that mercy pleasing in his sight which gives the people leisure to be mindful of him."[3]

Upon this statement follows the author's answer to the plea of the king. The latter, wishing to enjoy that kind of freedom which the removal of the guardian

---

[1] Or commonwealth.

[2] Cf. Et reformetur status regni nostri secundum quod melius viderent expedire ad honorem Dei, et ad fidem nostram, etc. Rymer, I., p. 373. Sel. Chart., p. 381.   [3] Lines 613, 614.

barons can alone establish, falls into a double error. The first is a misapprehension of the relation which his counsellors bear to himself. It is God alone, omniscient and omnipotent, who rules the universe in pure majesty, who alone cannot err or be vanquished by his enemies. He excels all earthly kings, his ministers, in that they cannot by their own unaided wisdom, or their own unaided strength, administer and defend the state. Counsellors are indispensable to them. The king must assent to this, yet requires absolute power over the selection of his helpers, asserting that otherwise he is not free but bound. Herein lies his second error, — a misapprehension of the nature of true liberty. "All constraint does not deprive of liberty, nor does every restriction take away power."[1] A true law, by preserving a king from a false law, increases his power, even as the might of angels is the greater because it is impossible for them ever to apostatize. "That a king is all powerful for good but dare work no evil," is God's special gift to him,[2] and it is in the enjoyment of this gift that his counsellors establish him and thus preserve his liberty. When a king rules himself and his kingdom rightly, then only is he truly free. All things whatsoever which advantage the kingdom are possible to him, but none which tend to its injury. To destroy by resisting the law is one thing: to rule according to the duty of a king is another and far nobler. "A ligando dicitur lex."

---

[1] Lines 667, 668.   [2] Lines 687, 688.

The discussion of the true relations which subsist between a king, his council, and his people is really a continuation of the poet's refutation of the royal argument. With inexorable logic it is shown that every king is the servant of God, and that no obedience is due to a king who is himself unfaithful to the service of his Master. That service is seeking God's glory in reigning, not the satisfaction of personal pride in despising one's peers.[1] The subjects of the king are not his, but God's, and they are meant to be the monarch's profitable helpers. "Let him make himself as one of them"[2] and love them. If a prince cherishes his people, they will not let him suffer wrong and he will in turn be loved by them; if he reigns justly, they perforce must honour him. If a prince errs, he should be checked by those whom his injustice has afflicted — unless he himself will correct his mistake. In that case they should raise him up and help him.

> Ipsam princeps teneat regulum regnandi,
> Ut opus non habeat non suos vocandi.[3]

A wise prince will never reject his people, but an unwise ruler will disturb his kingdom.[4] If, then, a prince is less wise than he should be, and yet insists on exercising his independent judgment, his realm will suffer harm.

> Igitur communitas regni consulatur.[5]

---

[1] Lines 701-708.   [2] Line 713.
[3] Lines 735, 736.   [4] Lines 757, 758.
[5] Line 765.

The king's best counsellors are men of native race; they best understand their own laws, know their operation by experience, and have a direct interest in their maintenance which aliens lack. That wise and just and useful men should administer the state is the concern of the community at large. The king's analogy from the freedom of the earls to his own is next answered, and, by implication, turned against himself. If individuals err, they are under the law and the law is enforced, or should be, lest the strength of the kingdom be foolishly wasted.

Finally comes the conclusion of the whole matter.[1] First in rank stands the community.

Præmio præferimus universitatem.[2]

Law reigns supreme over the dignity of the king and is his guide and stay; its absence overthrows the kingdom.[3] The maxim so often cited, "ut rex vult, lex vadit," is untrue — "nam lex stat, rex cadit." The sum of this universal, sovereign law is Truth, Charity, and Zeal for Salvation: let all royal ordinances be consonant with these; then will the people prosper, and the king's will indeed be law. No provision which is in accordance with this Trinity can disinherit the king by depriving him of his ancestral rights, for this Trinity is itself but the rightful norm of his actions. Law is unending, *eadem semper*. No beneficial change of cus-

---

[1] Part V., lines 847 to the end.
[2] Line 847.
[3] Line 864.

tom, however late it may occur, can therefore be rightly censured as an innovation or encroachment.

The king's private interest must always yield to that of the community; it is for their sake, not his own, that he has been ordained as ruler. The name of king is relative, and it implies protection. If he accomplish the salvation of the kingdom, he plays his part as king; but the king who busies himself with his own affairs exclusively is ignorant of the duties of the royal office.[1]

Even were a king all-wise, he should none the less impart his plans to his faithful friends, as Christ to the disciples, for they are his necessary agents. It is therefore evident that it becomes a king to take counsel with his nobles concerning the governance of the realm and the preservation of its peace; it is also fitting that natives, not foreigners, be his companions and advisers, for aliens abolish good customs and sow discord through the land. The king should uphold the rank of his natural subjects and thereby have joy in reigning. If, however, he shows himself studious to degrade them and debase their rank, he will seek in vain for an obedience which would be the part of fools.

So ends the remarkable poem of a thirteenth-century scholar. In the absence of an absolutely certain translation of the word "communitas," it is perhaps impossible to measure accurately the extent of the democratic

---

[1] Cf. Mat. Par., V., p. 614 (1257). Henry's reply to Edward, asking for help in the Welsh War. "Me autem alia negotia detinent occupatum." *Vide supra*, p. 147.

doctrines which the poem contains. This is particularly true of that essential portion which treats of the constitution of the governing council.

<blockquote>Igitur communitas regni consulatur.</blockquote>

It seems scarcely possible that a philosopher who by sheer dint of reason has discovered that the king is not above the law, that resistance is a duty if he violates it, that the law never changes although human perception of it does, and that the law is established primarily for the welfare of the nation, —

<blockquote>Præmio præferimus universitatem —</blockquote>

should then proceed to interpret "communitas regni" as the "community of the magnates." This interpretation seems still more absurd when we reflect that the author of the poem is undoubtedly a Minorite and therefore endowed with not only theoretical but also practical sympathy for the commons of the realm; that his reasoning is evidently based on the observation of actual political occurrences, and that he must have noted the very patent increase of the political power of the knighthood and of the city-communes in general, together with the decisive part played by the commune of London during the past three years. Moreover, but this is of course conjectural, the writ for the parliament of 1265 may have been issued before the completion of the poem and may have been seen by the author. It is scarcely probable that a poem so long, so artistically constructed, and involving such a wealth of political wisdom, could have been written in a very short space of time. The truth of the matter probably is, that the word "communitas" was at this very time undergoing a change of signification which would ultimately restrict its political meaning to the "Commons"; that in the line

> Igitur communitas regni consulatur

it is used by the author himself without any definite attempt to determine its exact connotation and denotation, but that he certainly would have included in it all authorized representatives of the people — the barons by birth, standing, and immemorial right, the knighthood by influence and ripening custom. Coupled with the poet's broadly democratic convictions, and his explicit statements that the interests of the commonwealth are paramount, that our knowledge of the fundamental law is progressive, and that political actions in accordance with our increased knowledge are not innovations, this line might well be indicative of a desire for the establishment of the broadest possible basis for the national council. The coincidence of the time of writing with the great political event of the half-century cannot fail to exercise great weight in behalf of this point of view. The poem certainly establishes theoretical conclusions broad enough to justify the representation of the higher classes of the commonalty in the central council of the nation; it is therefore quite within the bounds of possibility that the author himself may have had that idea more or less consciously in mind, and that his exposition of the relation of the voice of the people to the discovery of political truth approaches very near the maxim "Vox populi vox Dei."

In how far did Simon de Montfort share the doctrines of the poet? Did his theory keep pace with his practice, or was his political action, which forms almost the sole standard of our judgment, based wholly on practical insight, the drift of the times, and his own needs? These questions can scarcely be answered. We know that he received his sympathetic education largely through his intimacy with the leading Minorites, and there exists at least one definite proof that they had speculations in common on such subjects.[1] We also know by means of a direct assertion that he was well equipped in literary knowledge.[2] As a matter of individual opinion, then, one may be permitted to believe that de Montfort's political practice was based partly upon political theory; the belief is certainly not inconsistent with any known facts, and there is considerable pleasure in the thought that the man who did so much for the popular liberties of England, and who, according to the view of so many of his contemporaries, fell a martyr to his duty, the cause of God and the church, died in the light of a dawning faith that the voice of the people was indeed the voice of God.

"Inter arma silent leges:" not so of constitutions. The Barons' War was essentially a war of principles, and its permanent results lay along the line of constitu-

---

[1] Mon. Fran., Ep. Ad., XXV., p. 110.

[2] Rish., Chronicon, p. 6. Litteraturæ scientia commendabiliter præditus.

tional progress. The Provisions of Oxford were in advance of those of Runnymede in so far as they were a legitimate elaboration of the latter's fundamental principles, sought to establish a system of administration which would ensure the observance of the Charters as against the king himself, and laid a stress unknown before upon the inalienable rights of native Englishmen and upon the unity of England. The Barons' War advanced the constitution immeasurably farther, through the spread of democratic doctrines and the admission of new classes to the exercise of governmental functions. It established the liberties of England not only upon a national, but a popular basis.

With this latter chain of progression the name of Simon de Montfort is inextricably interlinked. His reluctance [1] to sign the Provisions of Oxford may have been due to disapproval of the cumbrousness of the executive organization, or to a belief that the basis of the constitution was too narrow. He certainly favoured both the ordinance of the year 1258 which extended to vassals the same privileges which the king accorded to their lords, and also the provisions of 1259 which were wrung from the barons by the unrepresented knighthood of the realm. Out of four known writs [2] which, prior to 1265, summoned knights to represent their counties in the national parliament, two

---

[1] Lanercost, p. 67.
[2] I., Nov. 7, 1213. II., 1254. III., 1261. Sel. Chart., pp. 405, 406. Shirley, II., p. 179. IV., June 4, 1264. Rymer, I., p. 442. The last two are Simon's.

were due to de Montfort. He was the pride of the Minorites, the heralds of the popular movement, and the idol of the commune of London. The crowning act of his career was the construction of the parliament of 1265, with its rich freightage for all coming years. His sudden removal from the scene of action seemed to destroy in a moment the labours of a life; but the aspiration of one age proved to be the promise of fulfilment in the next, and the force of his one supreme creative act was never lost.

The true culmination of the national movement in the reign of Henry III. was reached in the sphere of thought when the poet in his silent chamber realized that the royal power was limited by the divine will, that the divine will was exercised for the welfare of all people on the earth, whatever their rank or station, and that of this will the community was the true interpreter; it was reached in the sphere of action when the founder of the House of Commons withdrew this thought from the realm of the abstract, and gave it concrete existence by giving to the people of England a share in the exercise of sovereign power.

www.ingramcontent.com/pod-product-compliance
Lightning Source LLC
Chambersburg PA
CBHW032223230426
43666CB00033B/895